CONTENTS

KU-725-906

	Page
How to use this guide	1
Addresses of United Kingdom repositories mentioned in the guide	2
Printed sources	3
Abbreviations used	3
Acknowledgements	3
Part I: Introduction to the sources	4
Records of English baptisms, marriages and burials in churches and chapels overseas	4
'International memoranda' of baptisms, marriages and burials overseas, at Guildhall Library	6
Civil registration records of births, marriages and deaths of English residents in foreign countries (from 1849), at the Office of Population Censuses and Surveys	6
Civil registration records in Empire and Commonwealth countries	7
Foreign Office records at the Public Record Office, Kew	8
Non-statutory records at the Public Record Office, Chancery Lane	8
Records of military units abroad and ships at sea	9
Records of the Scots, Irish and Welsh overseas	11
Other related sources	12
Emigration records	12
Wills	13
Monumental inscriptions	13
Obituaries	13
The Mormon International Genealogical Index	13
The Society of Genealogists	13
Sources available outside the United Kingdom	14
Part II: List of known registers for individual places overseas	16-110

THE BRITISH OVERSEAS

a guide to records
of their births, baptisms,
marriages, deaths and burials,
available in the United Kingdom

GUILDHALL LIBRARY
THIRD (REVISED) EDITION
1994

Guildhall Library Publications
Guildhall Library, Aldermanbury, London.

ISBN 0 900422 39 4

First published 1984
Second edition 1988
Third (revised) edition 1995

Copyright © Guildhall Library

Printed in Britain by
Manor Park Press Limited, England.

8/94-PSB 5453

Cover illustration: entries from a register of baptisms, marriages and burials
in St Petersburg, 1763 (Guildhall Library, Ms 11192B)

HOW TO USE THIS GUIDE

What it includes

This *Guide* is to sources which may be used to trace the births (or baptisms), marriages and deaths (or burials) of British persons overseas, occurring before c.1945. Some post-1945 sources are mentioned, but for more detailed information about this period enquiries should be made to the Office of Population Censuses and Surveys at St Catherine's House, 10 Kingsway, London WC2B 6JP for personal searches and at the General Register Office, Smedley Hydro, Birkdale, Southport PR8 2HH for postal applications.

The *Guide* is primarily to sources available in the United Kingdom. Some material held in other countries is mentioned, but no attempt has been made at comprehensive coverage.

How to trace a particular person or family

1. Consult list of sources for individual countries (pages 16-110).
2. If this does not provide the information required, consult, as appropriate:
   (a) English and Welsh civil registration records of births, marriages and deaths in foreign countries (i.e. outside the British Empire or Commonwealth), from 1849, at the Office of Population Censuses and Surveys (see pages 6-7); or similar Scottish and Irish civil registration records (see page 11).
   (b) 'Miscellaneous' series 1826-1951 at the Public Record Office, Chancery Lane (see pages 8-9).
   (c) Various sources for events at sea and persons serving in military units abroad (see pages 9-10).
3. If more guidance is needed, read the detailed introduction to the background and nature of the sources (pages 4-15).
4. If the above sources do not provide the information required, it will be necessary to search for records held outside the United Kingdom (see pages 14-15).

ADDRESSES OF UNITED KINGDOM REPOSITORIES MENTIONED IN THE GUIDE

Borthwick Institute of Historical Research, St Anthony's Hall, Peasholme Green, York YO1 2PW.

British Library, Great Russell Street, London WC1B 3DG.

Church Missionary Society, 157 Waterloo Road, London SE1 8UU.

Genealogical Libraries of the Church of Jesus Christ of Latter-Day Saints: Hyde Park Family History Centre, Church of Jesus Christ of Latter-Day Saints, 64-8 Exhibition Road, London SW7 2PA (and other addresses in various countries).

Greater London Record Office, 40 Northampton Road, London EC1R 0HB.

Guildhall Library, Aldermanbury, London EC2P 2EJ.

India Office Library: British Library, Oriental and India Office collections, 197 Blackfriars Road, London SE1 8NG.

Lambeth Palace Library, London SE1 7JU.

Methodist Missionary Society: archives held in the Library of the School of Oriental and African Studies, Thornhaugh Street, Russell Square, London WC1H 0XG.

National Library of Scotland, George IV Bridge, Edinburgh EH1 1EW.

New College Library, Edinburgh: enquiries should be addressed to Edinburgh University Library, Special Collections Department, George Square, Edinburgh EH8 9LJ.

Office of Population Censuses and Surveys at St Catherine's House, 10 Kingsway, London WC2B 6JP for personal searches and at the General Register Office, Smedley Hydro, Birkdale, Southport PR8 2HH for postal searches.

Principal Probate Registry (Principal Registry of the Family Division), Somerset House, Strand, London WC2R 1LP.

Public Record Office, Chancery Lane, London WC2A 1LR.*

Public Record Office, Ruskin Avenue, Kew, Surrey TW9 4DU.*

Scottish Record Office, HM General Register House, Princes Street, Edinburgh EH1 3YY.

Society for Promoting Christian Knowledge, Holy Trinity Church, Marylebone Road, London NW1 4DU.

Society of Genealogists, 14 Charterhouse Buildings, Goswell Road, London EC1M 7BA.

United Society for the Propagation of the Gospel: archives held in the Rhodes House Library, South Parks Road, Oxford OX1 3RG.

---

*The Public Record Office will be united on the Kew site from the beginning of 1997. Serious disruption to the service is likely from the end of 1994. Readers are strongly advised to contact the Public Record Office in advance of a visit.

PRINTED SOURCES

Printed books and other publications mentioned in the *Guide* are available for consultation at Guildhall Library unless otherwise stated. They can also generally be seen at the Society of Genealogists and/or the British Library.

ABBREVIATIONS USED

Bap:	baptism(s)	Mar:	marriage(s)
Bur:	burial(s)	PRO:	Public Record Office
c.:	circa	Vol:	volume(s)

ACKNOWLEDGEMENTS

The British Overseas was originally compiled by Geoffrey Yeo and first published in 1984. It was revised by the author in 1986 with a second edition being published in 1988.

The considerable achievement of Geoffrey Yeo has been augmented and brought up to date in this third revised edition. I am grateful to the many people who have assisted in the revision of the *Guide*, including the staff of most of the repositories holding overseas registers.

The holdings of Guildhall Library are described as at 1 August 1994 and those of other repositories from information supplied between 27 September 1993 and 1 August 1994.

Philippa White
1 August 1994

PART I
INTRODUCTION TO THE SOURCES
RECORDS OF ENGLISH BAPTISMS, MARRIAGES AND BURIALS IN CHURCHES AND CHAPELS OVERSEAS

Churches in non-English-speaking countries

Anglican churches were established in many European towns from the 17th century onwards. In some towns English non-conformist churches were also established. Before this, in France, Germany, the Netherlands and Switzerland, the baptisms, marriages and burials of Anglican and English non-conformist residents were commonly recorded in the registers of local protestant churches. This practice probably continued at later dates in areas where there was no convenient English church. It appears that such entries are particularly numerous in the protestant registers of Angers, Bordeaux, Caen, Nantes, Saumur, Tours, Basle, Frankfurt, Geneva, Rotterdam, Strasbourg and Zurich.* These registers are of course kept in their country of origin, usually at the church in question or in a local record repository. It is not known what arrangements were made by Anglicans and non-conformists in countries where there were no protestant churches. In some countries burials were performed secretly, often by laymen, and no registers or other records of the events were kept. English Roman Catholics overseas should be sought in the baptism, marriage and burial registers of local Roman Catholic churches.

When English churches were established in Europe, they began to maintain their own registers. One of the earliest known is that of the Anglican church at Hamburg, which begins in 1617**. A few other 17th century registers exist, but for most English churches in Europe the surviving records do not begin until the 18th or (more commonly) the 19th century.

There are also some registers for churches in non-English-speaking countries outside Europe, though few were established before the 19th century. It is not known what arrangements were made by English residents in countries where there was no English church. Some baptisms, marriages and burials may have been entered in the registers of other churches, while some are likely to have remained unrecorded.

Where Anglican or other 'English' churches existed overseas, they are likely to have been used on occasion by others besides English people. Thus the registers of Anglican churches may include baptisms, marriages and burials of Welsh, Scottish, Irish or colonial Anglicans. Mixed marriages (i.e. where one party was a foreign national), and baptisms of the children of such marriages, may be found either in local protestant or Roman Catholic registers or in those of Anglican or English non-conformist churches.

---

*J. S. Burn, *The History of Parish Registers* . . . (London, 1862), page 241; N. Currer-Briggs, *Worldwide Family History* (London, 1982), page 28; *National Index of Parish Registers,* vol 2 (Chichester, 1973), pages 763-7.

**A register was kept at Flushing (Vlissingen) from 1593, but was destroyed in a fire in 1809: W. Steven, *History of the Scottish Church, Rotterdam* (Edinburgh, 1832),.page 305 (not available at Guildhall Library).

Many Anglican registers have been forwarded to the United Kingdom for safe keeping (see below), but few records of non-conformist churches overseas are available for consultation here.

Churches in former British colonies

Anglican churches were established in overseas colonial territories from the 17th century onwards. However some clergy, especially in the early years of a colony, did not feel obliged to keep registers of the baptisms, marriages and burials which they performed. Registers of colonial churches were very rarely sent to England, and in most cases must be sought in the country concerned.

Records held in the United Kingdom

The records of overseas churches which are available for consultation in the United Kingdom fall into three categories: (a) original registers which have been brought to the United Kingdom; (b) copies made for official purposes, e.g. 'bishop's transcripts'; (c) published and unpublished transcripts or photographic copies made by researchers. Many Anglican registers in categories (a) and (b) are at Guildhall Library as part of the archives of the Bishop of London, who was held to exercise responsibility for Anglican churches overseas where no other bishop had been appointed;* further registers can be found at PRO Chancery Lane, Lambeth Palace Library and various other repositories. Details are given on pages 16-110.

Records held outside the United Kingdom

Considerable numbers of records remain in the custody of individual churches or in archive repositories overseas. Possible means of tracing them are suggested on pages 14-15. Some are mentioned on pages 16-110.

---

*For the origins and legal status of the Bishop of London's jurisdiction overseas, see the introduction to W. W. Manross, *The Fulham Papers in Lambeth Palace Library* (Oxford, 1965) and Geoffrey Yeo, 'A Case Without Parallel: the Bishops of London and the Anglican Church Overseas, 1660-1748', in *Journal of Ecclesiastical History* vol 44 (1993), pages 450-75. The Bishop of London retained responsibility for churches in north and central Europe until 1980, but his jurisdiction in southern Europe ceased in 1842 on the creation of the diocese of Gibraltar. The allegiance of the American (Episcopal) church to the Bishop of London came to an end after American independence in 1776. The first Anglican bishop in Canada was appointed in 1787, and the other British colonies generally acquired bishops of their own in the 19th century. This explains why registers from colonial territories are not generally found in the Bishop of London's archives. However records of baptisms, marriages and burials in India were returned to the civil authorities and are now at the India Office Library in London: see page 46.

'INTERNATIONAL MEMORANDA' OF BAPTISMS, MARRIAGES AND BURIALS OVERSEAS AT GUILDHALL LIBRARY

In the 19th and early 20th centuries the Bishop of London's registry maintained a series of volumes (now known as 'International memoranda') for the registration of miscellaneous foreign baptisms, marriages and burials. Most of the entries are for baptisms and marriages by chaplains officiating at British embassies abroad, but the series includes a number of other registrations made, e.g., by clergymen travelling overseas or on board ship.*

Registrations were sometimes accepted up to thirty years after a baptism, marriage or burial. Thus, although the first registration was accepted in 1816, the earliest baptism recorded in the series took place in 1788. The 'International memoranda' are Guildhall Library Ms 10926/1-13.

1. 1816-24	including baptisms, marriages & burials up to 30 years earlier	7. 1865-9	including baptisms, marriages & burials up to 5 years earlier	
2. 1824-32		8. 1869-72		
3. 1832-40		9. 1872-5		
4. 1840- 6		10. 1875-8		
5. 1847-57		11. 1878-83		
6. 1857-65		12. 1883-9		
		13. 1889-1924		

Ms 10926/1-10 may be consulted only on microfilm.

Indexes are kept on the open shelves in the Manuscripts reading room at Guildhall Library: Ms 10926C/1-2. For *details of the countries covered* in this series see pages 16-110.

From 1921 to 1969 the Bishop of Gibraltar likewise maintained a memorandum book for miscellaneous baptisms, some of them by clergymen travelling overseas on board ship*: Guildhall Library, Ms 23607.

An *index* is kept on the open shelves in the Manuscripts reading room at Guildhall Library: Ms 23607A. For *details of the countries covered* in this book see pages 16-110.

CIVIL REGISTRATION RECORDS OF BIRTHS, MARRIAGES AND DEATHS OF ENGLISH RESIDENTS IN FOREIGN COUNTRIES (FROM 1849), AT THE OFFICE OF POPULATION CENSUSES AND SURVEYS

The Acts of Parliament of 1836 and 1837, which established a system of civil registration of births, marriages and deaths in England and Wales, did not apply to persons of British nationality outside the United Kingdom. Statutory civil registration records of English births, marriages and deaths which occurred in foreign countries do not begin until 1849.** Since that date records of births and deaths which were known to British consuls and lega-

*For registrations at sea, see also pages 9-10.
**For Irish and Scottish births, marriages and deaths see page 11.

tions in foreign countries (i.e. outside the British Empire or Commonwealth) have been returned by them to the Registrar General, formerly in London, but now in Southport,* in accordance with Foreign Office instructions. Civil registration records of marriages solemnized or attended by British consuls in foreign countries are kept under the terms of the Consular Marriages Act 1849, and later enactments, which required that marriage registers should be maintained by each consul, and that certified copies thereof should be returned to the Registrar General. The Act of 1849 allowed for civil marriages to be conducted by the consuls themselves, but also covered marriages solemnized in the consul's presence by a clergyman of the Church of England or by any other person. Marriages conducted by a foreign minister under the marriage laws of the country concerned were known as *lex loci* marriages and were sometimes entered by consuls in separate registers; copies of these were also returned to the Registrar General. It is probable that many births, marriages and deaths in foreign countries, particularly in the 19th century, were unknown to the British consuls and were therefore not registered in this way; but the more recent records are likely to be more comprehensive.

Access to the records
All the above statutory (or 'consular') records of births, marriages and deaths in foreign countries are now kept with the Registrar General's civil registration records for England and Wales at the Office of Population Censuses and Surveys, General Register Office, Smedley Hydro, Birkdale, Southport PR8 2HH. The indexes to these records are held in the Public Search Room at St Catherine's House, 10 Kingsway, London WC2B 6JP. Postal enquiries should be directed to Southport and personal visits to St Catherine's House. Visitors to St Catherine's House can obtain information about overseas records from the Public Search Room staff, although the Overseas Registration Section is now at Southport. Members of the public can ask to speak to a member of the Overseas Registration Section while at St Catherine's House if the Public Search Room staff are unable to help. Certificates may be obtained on payment of the appropriate fee.

CIVIL REGISTRATION RECORDS IN EMPIRE AND COMMONWEALTH COUNTRIES

The records at the Office of Population Censuses and Surveys do not cover places which were part of the British Empire or Commonwealth at the time when the birth, marriage or death occurred. Residents in British colonies or dominions were subject to the registration laws in operation in the locality concerned, and records of their births, deaths and marriages were kept locally rather than being returned to London.

Possible means of tracing these records are suggested on page 14.

*In June 1991, the Registration Division of the Office of Population Censuses and Surveys relocated to Southport. Although all of the records previously held at St Catherine's House in London moved to Southport, the indexes to those records did not and are still held in the Public Search Room at St Catherine's House exactly as they were before. The Registrar General works in London, but all the returns now go to Southport where the records are kept.

FOREIGN OFFICE RECORDS AT THE PUBLIC RECORD OFFICE, KEW

A number of documents previously kept at British consulates abroad are available for public consultation among the Foreign Office records (class FO) at PRO Kew. These include some of the original registers of births, marriages and deaths from which the consuls' returns to the Registrar General were compiled. These original registers are therefore covered by the Registrar General's indexes. However the Public Record Office does not have copies of the indexes and researchers unsure of the place and date of registration, will need to consult the indexes held by the Office of Population Censuses and Surveys, at St Catherine's House before they look at the registers at the Public Record Office. It should also be noted that the registers do not represent the whole of the coverage of the Registrar General's records of overseas registration held by the Office of Population Censuses and Surveys.

The Foreign Office records also contain a number of registers of baptisms and burials, whose contents are apparently not duplicated elsewhere; and much other material relating to British residents overseas, including registers of passports issued at consulates, lists of British subjects in various towns overseas, and papers relating to the wills and estates of British expatriates, mainly from the late 19th and early 20th centuries.

Details of the Foreign Office registers of births, baptisms, marriages, deaths and burials held in embassy and consular archives at PRO Kew (including those whose contents are duplicated at the Office of Population Censuses and Surveys) are given in the list on pages 16-110 of this *Guide*. For other Foreign Office material the enquirer is advised to consult the *Current Guide to the Contents of the Public Record Office* (PRO microfiche publication) and the typewritten lists in the search rooms at PRO Kew (some of which have been published by the Kraus Reprint Corporation, New York, various dates). Access to the records is subject to a 30-year (in some cases 50-year) closure period.

Some non-consular registers have also been included in the list on pages 16-110 of this *Guide*. There is no complete list of records of births, baptisms, marriages, deaths and burials held by the Public Record Office, and there may well be other records at PRO Kew which contain information relating to overseas registration.

NON-STATUTORY RECORDS AT THE PUBLIC RECORD OFFICE, CHANCERY LANE

Besides the statutory records described on pages 6-7, the Registrar General also had custody of a number of non-statutory registers of births, baptisms, marriages, deaths and burials overseas received from the Bishop of London. In 1977 these were transferred to PRO Chancery Lane, where they form five series known as 'Miscellaneous Foreign Returns' (RG32), 'Foreign Registers and Returns' (RG33), 'Miscellaneous Foreign Marriages' (RG34), 'Miscellaneous Foreign Deaths' (RG35) and 'Registers and Returns of Births, Marriages and Deaths in Protectorates etc . . .' (RG36).

Each of the registers in RG33 relates to a particular locality, and details of the places and dates covered are given in the list on pages 16-110. Details of RG36 will also be found on pages 16-110. Indexes to RG33 and RG36 are kept on the open shelves at PRO Chancery Lane.

The 'Miscellaneous' series 1826-1951
The 'Miscellaneous' registers which comprise RG32, RG34 and RG35 contain numerous entries from all parts of the world between 1826 and 1951, and their contents have not been analysed in detail on pages 16-110. Most of the entries are from 'foreign' countries, but some Empire and Commonwealth registrations are included. Indexes to entries made before 1946 (except military deaths 1914-21) are also kept at PRO Chancery Lane, as follows:

Births & bap 1831-1930: RG43/2 Deaths & bur 1830-81: RG43/4
Mar 1826-1916: RG43/8   Deaths & bur 1881-1900: RG43/5
Mar 1913-20: RG43/9   Deaths & bur 1901-20: RG43/6
Births, bap, mar, deaths & bur 1921-45: RG43/10-14.

RECORDS OF MILITARY UNITS ABROAD AND SHIPS AT SEA*

The Army and Royal Air Force
Records of births, marriages and deaths (also some baptisms and burials) in Army regiments at home and abroad are held by the Office of Population Censuses and Surveys.** The records cover 1761-date for regiments based in England, but the earliest overseas entry is c.1790. From 1920 entries relating to the Royal Air Force are also included. The records are known as 'Regimental registers', with additional series known as 'Army returns' and 'Chaplains' returns'.

A few further records of baptisms, marriages and burials by Forces' chaplains abroad are held elsewhere, including:

Cape of Good Hope garrison, bap 1795-1803, mar 1796-1803, bur 1795-1803: Guildhall Library, Ms 11569.

Germany, British Army on the Rhine, civilian bap 1949-61 and 1969-76: Guildhall Library, Ms 11225-5B.

Gibraltar garrison, bap and mar 1807-12, bur 1807: Guildhall Library, Ms 10446D.

Palestine forces, bap 1939-47, banns 1944-7: PRO Kew, WO156/6-8.

Some military baptisms, marriages and burials may be entered in non-military registers (for which see pages 16-110).

Ships at sea (Merchant vessels and Royal Navy)
Births and deaths on board merchant vessels may be recorded in the log of the ship concerned. However few ships' logs survive from before the mid

*For wills of soldiers and sailors see page 13.

**The garrison registers listed on pages 185-6 of *Abstract of arrangements respecting registration of births, marriages and deaths in the United Kingdom and the other countries of the British Commonwealth* . . . (HMSO, 1952) form part of these records. Some names from the garrison registers appear in the index volumes kept at PRO Chancery Lane but the registers themselves remain with the Office of Population Censuses and Surveys.

19th century. Some are at PRO Kew, but it is practicable to search them only if the name of the ship is known.

However from 1837 to date records of English births and deaths at sea returned by captains of merchant vessels and Royal Navy ships are held by the Office of Population Censuses and Surveys.* These records are indexed. They are known as 'Marine births' and 'Marine deaths'. There are also records of births 1854-91, marriages 1854-83 and deaths 1854-90 of seamen and passengers on merchant ships at PRO Kew (class BT 158-60). Later records are held by the Registrar General of Shipping and Seamen, Block 2, Government Buildings, St Agnes Road, Gabalfa, Cardiff CF4 4XA. Marriages 1842-89 on Royal Navy ships are recorded at PRO Chancery Lane (class RG33/156; index in RG43/7); for the period 1842-79 these marriages are also registered in the 'International memoranda' at Guildhall Library (see page 6).

Guildhall Library also has records of some baptisms and burials at sea 1894-1952 (Ms 11827), and baptisms at sea 1955-61 (Ms 11817; index in Ms 15061/1-2, under 'sea'). There are some further baptisms, 1810, 1822 and 1860-1921, and burials, 1860-1919, at sea in the 'International memoranda' at Guildhall Library (see page 6). Additional baptisms at sea are in the Bishop of Gibraltar's memorandum book of miscellaneous baptisms, 1921-69, at Guildhall Library (see page 6).

The popular belief that all baptisms at sea were registered at St Dunstan Stepney is incorrect**; however there are some baptisms at sea from 1893 entered in the registers of that church, which are held by the Greater London Record Office. The records there include baptisms for the Mediterranean fleet at Malta 1933-8.

Registers of baptisms and burials in the Naval dockyard at Bermuda 1826-1946 are at PRO Kew (class ADM 6).

War deaths
Deaths of military personnel overseas in the Boer War 1899-1902, First World War 1914-21 and Second World War 1939-48 are recorded and indexed by the Office of Population Censuses and Surveys. Printed sources which may also be relevant include, for the First World War, *The War Graves of the British Empire, 1914-18*, and for the Second World War, *The War Dead of the British Commonwealth, 1939-45*, both published by the Commonwealth War Graves Commission. Guildhall Library also has copies of the War Office's official lists of officers and soldiers who died in the First World War, arranged by regiment.

---

*For similar records relating to Irish and Scottish births and deaths see page 11.

**See A. D. Ridge, 'All at Sea', in *Archives* vol 6 (1964).

RECORDS OF THE SCOTS, IRISH AND WELSH OVERSEAS

A useful starting point for those interested in Scots overseas is Donald Whyte, *The Scots Overseas. A Selected Bibliography* (Birmingham, 1988). It gives details of several published lists of Scottish emigrants.

Church records
Baptisms, marriages and burials overseas of persons of Scottish, Irish or Welsh origin who were members of the Anglican church or of a British non-conformist sect (e.g. the Methodist church) should be sought in the records of the appropriate 'English' church, if there was one: see pages 4-5. Those who were members of the Roman Catholic church should be sought in the registers of local Roman Catholic churches in the country concerned.

Some records of Church of Scotland (Presbyterian) churches abroad have been returned to the United Kingdom: details are given in the list on pages 16-110. Information about other records should be sought from the churches themselves. The addresses of individual churches can be obtained from the Church of Scotland Overseas Council, 121 George Street, Edinburgh EH2 4YR.

Civil registration records: Scottish
Civil records of Scottish births and deaths overseas, and of marriages overseas where one or both parties were of Scottish origin, from 1860, and civil records of Scottish births and deaths at sea from 1855, are held at the General Register Office for Scotland, New Register House, Edinburgh EH1 3YT.

Civil registration records: Irish
Civil records of Irish births and deaths certified by British consuls abroad, and of Irish births and deaths at sea, 1864-1921, are held at the General Register Office, 8-11 Lombard Street East, Dublin 2. Similar records for Northern Irish births and deaths, commencing in 1922, are at the General Register Office Northern Ireland, Oxford House, Chichester Street, Belfast BT1 4HL.

Civil registration records: Welsh
There are no separate civil records of Welsh births, marriages and deaths overseas. They are included in the records of English civil registration described on pages 6-7.

OTHER RELATED SOURCES

Emigration records

The Public Record Office (Kew and Chancery Lane) has a large number of unpublished sources relating to emigration from Britain, particularly emigration to North America, the West Indies, Australia and New Zealand in the 18th and 19th centuries. Records relating to the transportation of convicts from Britain are also held there. A leaflet giving details of these sources is available at the Public Record Office.

Surviving records of immigrants at foreign ports of arrival are generally kept in the National Archives in the country concerned. Its address can usually be obtained from the latest edition of *The World of Learning* (Europa Publications, London). In some countries, notably Australia and South Africa, immigration records are kept in State or Provincial Archives.

A number of emigrant ship passenger lists, and lists of early settlers in the American, South African and Australasian colonies, have been published. For the United States, Canada and the West Indies, P. William Filby, *et al* (ed.s), *Passenger and immigration lists index* and *Passenger and immigration lists bibliography 1538-1900* (Detroit, 1981-94) will be found especially useful. The Society of Genealogists has a large collection of published work of this kind (for Australasia and South Africa as well as America). A number of published works are also available at Guildhall Library.

Several indexes relating to emigration and transportation are available in the United Kingdom. The F. L. Leeson Emigrant Index, 1600-1855, compiled from a wide variety of printed and manuscript sources, concerns emigrants to America, the West Indies and Canada. Full details are available from Debrett Ancestry Research Limited, PO Box 7, Alresford, Hampshire SO24 9EN.

An index to those transported to Australia, Tasmania or Western Australia, 1787-1868, has been compiled by Miss J. M. Chambers, 54 Chagny Close, Letchworth, Hertfordshire SG6 4BY. The index includes information from the following sources: Convict Transportation Registers at PRO Chancery Lane (class HO11); Male Convict Registers and some Male Convict Description Lists at the Tasmanian Archive Office (CON31); and Convict Indents, 1788-1842, Registers of Convict Applications to Marry, 1826-51 and Convict Deaths, 1828-79 at the New South Wales Archives Office.

A separate index to Convict Indents in New South Wales, Australia, 1788-1842, compiled by the Genealogical Society of Victoria, is available at Guildhall Library (fiche 29) and the Institute of Heraldic and Genealogical Studies, Northgate, Canterbury, Kent CT1 1BA.

Miss Chambers has also compiled an index to Parish Assisted Emigrants, 1834-60, chiefly from Poor Law records at PRO Chancery Lane (class MH12) and, for some counties, cross-referenced to county record office records. Destinations include the United States of America, Canada, Australia, Tasmania, New Zealand and South Africa.

An index of assisted immigrants to Australia, 1839-71, is included in *Victoria, Public Record Office, British Immigration to Victoria Resource Kit, Stage 1, Assisted Immigrants from the UK, 1839-71* (Victoria, 1988) available at Guildhall Library (fiche 3).

Wills
Wills of Englishmen dying abroad or at sea but in possession of goods in England were generally proved, until 1858, in the Prerogative Court of Canterbury. The records of this court are at PRO Chancery Lane; they include wills of soldiers and sailors besides those of civilians dying abroad.

Such wills were occasionally proved, until 1858, in other courts. The will of an individual dying abroad whose property was wholly within one English diocese may sometimes be found in the records of a probate court in that diocese: for a list of such courts and their records see A. Camp, *Wills and their Whereabouts* (London, 1974). The records of the Prerogative Court of York, held at the Borthwick Institute of Historical Research in York, also include many persons dying abroad with property in the north of England.

Enquiries about wills of persons dying abroad with property in England after 1858 should be made to the Principal Probate Registry at Somerset House.

Wills of persons dying abroad with property in Scotland are to be found in the records of the Commissariat of Edinburgh. These records (pre-1960) are at the Scottish Record Office.

From the late 17th century there are many wills of seamen on merchant vessels (to 1857), and some on ships of the Royal Navy (to c.1750), in the records of the Commissary Court of London (London division) at Guildhall Library. These records also include some wills of soldiers dying abroad (c.1790-c.1830).

Original wills of seamen in the Royal Navy 1786-1882 are at PRO Kew (class ADM48).

Monumental inscriptions
A number of transcripts of inscriptions from graveyards overseas exist in published or unpublished form. The largest collection is at the Society of Genealogists. A number are also available at Guildhall Library.

Obituaries
An index of Britons dying outside the British Isles from the 16th century is being compiled by D. Pearce, Wayside, Roman Road, Twyford, Winchester, Hampshire SO21 1QW. For a search send a stamped addressed envelope and five second class stamps in the United Kingdom or three International Reply Coupons for overseas enquiries.

The Mormon International Genealogical Index
This index, compiled by the Church of Jesus Christ of Latter-Day Saints, includes numerous persons baptised and married in many countries throughout the world. There is a separate part of the index for each country. The parts for countries outside the British Isles are not available at Guildhall Library, but may be seen at the Society of Genealogists or at the Genealogical Libraries of the Church of Jesus Christ of Latter-Day Saints.

The Society of Genealogists
The Society of Genealogists holds numerous books and periodicals relating

to various aspects of overseas genealogy and the activities of English communities abroad. Many of them are not readily available elsewhere in the United Kingdom. By no means all contain biographical details about named individuals, but even those which do not may be found useful in providing background information and in suggesting further lines of enquiry.

SOURCES AVAILABLE OUTSIDE THE UNITED KINGDOM

Records held by civil registration authorities

Civil registration records of births, marriages and deaths kept locally outside the United Kingdom may include details of British residents in the country concerned. Details of such records kept in Commonwealth countries can be found in *Abstract of arrangements respecting registration of births, marriages and deaths in the United Kingdom and the other countries of the British Commonwealth . . .* (HMSO, 1952). The addresses of some registration authorities have changed since the publication of *Abstract of arrangements . . .,* and a more up-to-date list of their addresses can be found in *Fees for searches and certificates of events occurring outside England and Wales* (General Register Office, 1967). This booklet is not available at Guildhall Library, but an annotated copy can be seen on request at the Office of Population Censuses and Surveys, at St Catherine's House. The staff of the Overseas Registration Section at the Office of Population Censuses and Surveys, General Register Office, Smedley Hydro, Birkdale, Southport PR8 2HH can also supply the current addresses of registration authorities in non-Commonwealth countries, and advise on the procedure for making enquiries to these authorities (postal applications only).

Civil registration was introduced at different times in different countries overseas. In most countries the records go back to the 19th century but in some countries civil registration was not introduced, or made comprehensive, until the 20th century. However in a number of countries the civil registration authorities are also able to provide information about church registers and any other sources which pre-date the introduction of civil registration.

Records held in archive repositories

In some countries church registers are now in the custody of public archive repositories. Such repositories are most likely to have custody of the records of those churches to which the bulk of the local population belonged. Records of 'English' churches in non-English-speaking countries are less likely to be found in archive repositories abroad. However such repositories may be able to provide information about the whereabouts of surviving church registers even if these are not in their own custody.

The addresses of National Archives in overseas countries can usually be obtained from the latest edition of *The World of Learning* (Europa Publications, London). However church registers are often held in provincial, state or other local repositories, whose addresses should be sought from the

National Archives or from the London embassy or high commission of the country concerned.

Records held in churches
Many churches overseas retain custody of their own registers, and in such cases information should be sought from the incumbent or minister of the church in question. A booklet giving addresses of Anglican and other English churches in Europe, North Africa and the Middle East can be purchased from the Intercontinental Church Society, 175 Tower Bridge Road, London SE1 2AQ. Details of registers held in Anglican Chaplaincies within the Diocese of Gibraltar in Europe, where known to Guildhall Library, are given in the list on pages 16-110 of this *Guide*. For Anglican churches outside Europe, North Africa and the Middle East addresses may be obtainable from the diocesan authorities in the country concerned; details of Anglican dioceses overseas can be found in the latest edition of *The Church of England Year Book* (CIO Publishing, London). Similar publications are available for most other major denominations. They are not held at Guildhall Library but may be consulted nearby at the City Business Library, 1 Brewers' Hall Garden, London EC2V 5BX, and at many other public reference libraries. It should be noted, however, that an enquiry to the church authorities about a particular baptism, marriage or burial, is unlikely to be successful if the church where it took place is not known to the enquirer.

PART II

LIST OF KNOWN REGISTERS FOR INDIVIDUAL PLACES OVERSEAS

With some exceptions, this list refers only to registers of British communities overseas which are available for consultation in the United Kingdom. It is arranged alphabetically by name of country, such names being given as far as possible in the form in common English use after the end of the Second World War, with cross-references from earlier or later names. Names of cities and towns are indicated where possible (though the register for a city or town is likely to include surrounding villages, and frequently a much wider area); dedications of churches are not given. In most cases no attempt has been made to distinguish unpublished transcripts from original registers.

Under each place, registers are listed chronologically in the following order: births/baptisms, marriages and deaths/burials; general registers are listed first.

Dates given in the list are generally covering dates only. It is rarely clear whether gaps in a series represent periods when no registrations were made, or are the result of loss or neglect. In some instances the dates given may be those when births, etc., were registered by an appropriate authority; in such cases the birth itself may have taken place at an earlier date. When an overlap of covering dates is found in the list, it will be advisable to examine all the sources mentioned, as there were often separate registers kept by different officials or clergymen in the same locality.

The list includes all the overseas registers held by the Society of Genealogists, not only those which relate to British communities overseas. Where registers obviously relate to other nationalities, this is indicated in the list. A more detailed analysis is available at the Society of Genealogists.

The list does not include the statutory 'consular' registers 1849-date (see pages 6-7 and 11); and does not give a full analysis of the 'miscellaneous' series 1826-1951 at PRO Chancery Lane (see page 9), or of the various general series for military units abroad and ships at sea (see pages 9-10). Some non-consular registers at PRO Kew have been included in the list, but coverage may not be comprehensive (see page 8).

ADEN (SOUTH YEMEN)

Births, mar and deaths 1839-43: printed in *East India Register* 1840-4 (under 'Bombay').

Births, mar and deaths 1839-82: printed in *Bombay Directory* 1840-83 (not available at Guildhall Library).

Bap, mar and bur 1840-1969: India Office Library, N/13/1-21.

For addresses of repositories see page 2

For other sources which may relate to places on this page see 'How to use this guide' (page 1)

ALGERIA

Many entries among registrations for France and its colonies in 'Miscellaneous' series 1826-1951 at PRO Chancery Lane (see page 9).

Some entries for bap post 1920 in the Bishop of Gibraltar's memorandum book at Guildhall Library: see page 6.

ANGOLA

Luanda
Births 1865-1906, mar 1871-1928, deaths 1859-1906: PRO Kew, FO375/1-4.

ANGUILLA: see WEST INDIES

ANTIGUA: see WEST INDIES

ARGENTINA

General
Some entries for bap 1815-41, mar 1813-95 in 'International memoranda' at Guildhall Library: see page 6.

Buenos Aires
Bap and mar 1909-46: Society of Genealogists.
Mar 1826-1900: PRO Kew, FO446/3-6, 28-30.

ARUBA

Births 1930-62, deaths 1926-64: PRO Kew, FO907/12-21, 27-30, 38.

ASCENSION ISLAND

Bap 1839-61, mar 1840-59, deaths 1839-61: Society of Genealogists.
Bap 1846, mar 1847-56 in 'International memoranda' at Guildhall Library: see page 6.

AUSTRALIA

General
Microfiche copies of indexes to *New South Wales* bap 1790-1856, births 1856-99, mar 1789-1899 and bur 1787-1899; *Queensland* bap 1829-56, mar 1839-99, bur 1829-56 and deaths 1856-99; *South Australia* births, mar and deaths 1842-1906; *Victoria* births, mar and deaths 1837-95; *Western Australia* births, mar and deaths 1841-96; are available at the Society of

---

For addresses of repositories see page 2

For other sources which may relate to places on this page see 'How to use this guide' (page 1)

Genealogists (see also below). The original records are held locally in Australia, and enquiries about them should be addressed to the Registrar of the appropriate Australian state, at the following addresses:

Australian Capital Territory: the Registrar of Births, Deaths and Marriages, PO Box 788, Canberra City, Australian Capital Territory 2601, Australia.

New South Wales: the Registry of Births, Deaths and Marriages, GPO Box 30, Sydney, New South Wales 2001, Australia.

Northern Territory: Darwin — the Deputy Registrar of Births, Deaths and Marriages, PO Box 3021, Darwin, Northern Territory 0801, Australia; Alice Springs — the District Registrar, Courthouse, PO Box 8043, Alice Springs, Northern Territory 0871, Australia.

Queensland: the Registrar General, PO Box 188, Brisbane North Quay, Queensland 4002, Australia.

South Australia: the Principal Registrar, GPO Box 1351, Adelaide, South Australia 5001, Australia.

Tasmania: the Registrar of Births, Deaths and Marriages, GPO Box 198, Hobart, Tasmania 7001, Australia.

Victoria: the Registrar of Births, Deaths and Marriages, PO Box 4332, Melbourne, Victoria 3001, Australia.

Western Australia: the Registrar General, PO Box 7720, Cloisters Square, Perth, Western Australia 6850, Australia.

The following State Houses in London also provide a service for certificates:

South Australia: the Agent-General for South Australia, 50 Strand, London WC2N 5LW.

Victoria: the Agent-General for Victoria, Victoria House, Melbourne Place, Strand, London WC2B 4LG.

For records of emigration to Australia see page 12.

For further information about Australian sources see Nick Vine Hall, *Tracing Your Family History in Australia, a Guide to Sources* (Rigby, 1985). Assistance may also be obtained from the Society of Australian Genealogists, Richmond Villa, 120 Kent Street, Sydney, New South Wales 2000, Australia.

New South Wales
Military bap 1817-24: Society of Genealogists
Index to births 1856-99, bap 1790-1856, mar 1789-1899, deaths 1856-99 and bur 1787-1899: Society of Genealogists.
Mar 1788-1800: Society of Genealogists.

For addresses of repositories see page 2

For other sources which may relate to places on this page see 'How to use this guide' (page 1)

New South Wales, Albury
Bap 1911 in 'International memoranda' at Guildhall Library: see page 6.

New South Wales, Burragorang
Roman Catholic bur 1855-1947: Society of Genealogists.

New South Wales, Cox's River
Roman Catholic bur 1873-1938: Society of Genealogists.

New South Wales, Sydney
Bap 1787, mar 1815-17, bur 1868-1912: Society of Genealogists.

Northern Territory
Index to alien births 1888-1922, deaths 1875-1922: Society of Genealogists.

Northern Territory, Anthony Lagoon
Index to deaths 1890-1949: Society of Genealogists.

Northern Territory, Darwin
Alien births 1888-1922, deaths 1875-1922 (indexed): Society of Genealogists.

Northern Territory, Katherine
Index to deaths 1887-1941: Society of Genealogists.

Northern Territory, New Castle Waters
Index to deaths 1893-1932: Society of Genealogists.

Queensland
Index to bap 1829-56, mar 1839-99, deaths 1856-99, bur 1829-56: Society of Genealogists.

Queensland, Brisbane
Index to mar 1856-99, deaths 1856-94: Society of Genealogists.
Mar 1868-72: Society of Genealogists.

Queensland, Moreton Bay
Index to births, mar and deaths 1846-60: Society of Genealogists.

Queensland, Mount Isa
Index to deaths c.1930-87: Society of Genealogists.

For addresses of repositories see page 2

For other sources which may relate to places on this
page see 'How to use this guide' (page 1)

South Australia
Index to births, mar 1842-1906, deaths 1842-1905: Society of Genealogists.

South Australia, Adelaide
Bap 1860-70, deaths 1840-2: Society of Genealogists.

South Australia, Morialta
Bap 1873-1920, mar 1873-1915: Society of Genealogists.

Tasmania, Hobart
Baptist bur 1835-86: Society of Genealogists.

Tasmania, Oatlands
Bur 1827-36: Society of Genealogists.

Tasmania, Sidmouth
Presbyterian bur 1840-1982: Society of Genealogists.

Victoria
Index to births 1837-95, bap 1896-1913, mar 1837-1913, deaths 1837-95: Society of Genealogists.

Victoria, Barry's Reef
Deaths 1894-1902: Society of Genealogists.

Victoria, Castlemaine
Presbyterian mar 1853-9: Society of Genealogists.

Western Australia
Index to births 1841-95, mar and deaths 1841-96: Society of Genealogists.

Western Australia, Bunbury
Bur 1839-52: Society of Genealogists.

AUSTRIA

General
Some entries for bap 1821-1902, mar 1849-91, bur 1849 in 'International memoranda' at Guildhall Library: see page 6.

Innsbruck
Bur 1957: Guildhall Library, in Ms 21477.

For addresses of repositories see page 2

For other sources which may relate to places on this page see 'How to use this guide' (page 1)

Trieste: see **ITALY**

Vienna
Mar 1883-91: PRO Kew, FO120/697.

AZORES: see PORTUGAL

BAHAMAS: see WEST INDIES

BALEARIC ISLANDS: see SPAIN

BANGLADESH: see INDIA

BARBADOS: see WEST INDIES

BELGIUM
General
Some entries for bap 1815-48, mar 1815-90 in 'International memoranda' at Guildhall Library: see page 6.
Many entries in 'Miscellaneous' series 1826-1951 at PRO Chancery Lane (see page 9); the series also includes separate death registers for Belgium 1830-71 (RG35/1-3) and 1914-21 (military deaths only; incomplete) (RG35/45-57).

Antwerp
Bap 1817-52, mar 1820-49, bur 1817-52: PRO Chancery Lane, RG33/1-2 (index to bap in RG43/1, mar in RG43/7, bur in RG43/3).
Bap 1819-30, mar 1821-30, bur 1819-30: Guildhall Library, Ms 11198 (index in Ms 15061/1-2).
Bap 1831-42, mar 1832-42, bur 1831-42: PRO Chancery Lane, in RG33/155 (index to bap in RG43/1, mar in RG43/7, bur in RG43/3).

Brussels
Bap, mar and bur 1818-26: Guildhall Library, Ms 11199 (index in Ms 15061/1-2).
Mar 1816-90: PRO Chancery Lane, RG33/3-8 (index in RG43/7).

Ghent
Bap 1865-73, mar 1865-71, bur 1865-73: Guildhall Library, Ms 29349.
Mar 1849-50: PRO Chancery Lane, RG33/9 (index in RG43/7).

For addresses of repositories see page 2

For other sources which may relate to places on this
page see 'How to use this guide' (page 1)

Liège
Bap 1823-5: Guildhall Library, in Ms 11219 (index in Ms 15061/1-2).

Ostend
Bap 1784-7, mar and bur 1784-6: Guildhall Library, Ms 10457/1 (index in Ms 15061/1-2).
Bap 1787-94: Guildhall Library, Ms 10457/2 (index in Ms 15061/1-2).
Mar 1787-94: Guildhall Library, Ms 10457/3 (index in Ms 15061/1-2).
Bur 1787-94: Guildhall Library, Ms 10457/4 (index in Ms 15061/1-2).
Military bap, mar and bur 1815-16: extracts printed in *The Genealogist* vol 1 (1877). The original vol from which these extracts were taken is now part of the Registrar General's military records held by the Office of Population Censuses and Surveys (see page 9).

BERMUDA
All known bap, mar and bur 1619-1826 recorded locally are indexed in A. C. Hollis Hallett, *Early Bermuda Records, a guide to the parish and clergy registers with some assessment lists and petitions* (Bermuda, 1991).
Bap, mar and bur 1619-26 (as above): Society of Genealogists.
Births, mar and deaths 1784-1914 recorded in Bermuda newspapers are indexed in C. F. E. Hollis Hallett, *Bermuda Index, 1784-1914, an index of births, marriages and deaths recorded in Bermuda newspapers* (Bermuda, 1989).
Births, mar and deaths 1784-1914 (as above): Society of Genealogists
Bap 1812-30, mar 1812-48, bur 1812-15: printed in *Miscellanea Genealogica et Heraldica* New series vol 4 (1884).
British naval dockyard bap and bur 1826-1946: PRO Kew, ADM6/434-6, 439.

Wills 1629-1835 are calendared and indexed in C. F. E. Hollis Hallett, *Early Bermuda Wills 1629-1835* (Bermuda, 1992)

Enquiries about other records (from 1619) should be addressed to the Bermuda Government Archives, Government Administration Building, 30 Parliament Street, Hamilton HM12, Bermuda.

BORNEO: see INDONESIA, NORTH BORNEO and SARAWAK

For addresses of repositories see page 2

For other sources which may relate to places on this page see 'How to use this guide' (page 1)

BRAZIL

General

Some entries for bap 1788 and 1813-47, mar 1815-89 in 'International memoranda' at Guildhall Library: see page 6.

Bahia

Bap 1821, bur 1821-2: Guildhall Library, in Ms 11217 (index in Ms 15061/1-2).

Mar 1816-20: PRO Chancery Lane, in RG33/155 (index in RG43/7).

Maranhao

Mar 1844: PRO Chancery Lane, in RG33/155 (index in RG43/7).

Morre Velho

Mar 1851-67: Office of Population Censuses and Surveys (index at PRO Chancery Lane, in RG43/7).

Para

Births and deaths 1840-1: PRO Chancery Lane, in RG33/155 (index to births in RG43/1, deaths in RG43/3).

Pernambuco

Bap, mar and bur 1838-44: Guildhall Library, in Ms 11217 (index in Ms 15061/1-2).

Recife

Bur 1822-1916: Society of Genealogists.

Rio de Janeiro

Bap, mar and bur 1840-4: Guildhall Library, Ms 11216 (index in Ms 15061/1-2).Births 1850-9: PRO Kew, FO743/11.
Births 1850-9: PRO Kew, FO743/11.
Mar 1809-18: PRO Chancery Lane, in RG33/155 (index in RG43/7).

São Paulo

Births 1932, mar 1933: PRO Kew, FO863/1-2.

For addresses of repositories see page 2

For other sources which may relate to places on this
page see 'How to use this guide' (page 1)

BRITISH GUIANA (GUYANA)

Colony of Demerara, Georgetown (Stabroek)
Bap 1798: Guildhall Library, in Ms 11569 (index in Ms 15061/1-2).
Bur extracts 1812-21: Society of Genealogists.

Colony of Essequibo
Bap 1821-8, mar 1827: United Society for the Propagation of the Gospel.

BULGARIA

General
Some entries for bap post 1920 in the Bishop of Gibraltar's memorandum book at Guildhall Library: see page 6.

Plovdiv (Philippopolis)
Births 1880-1922, deaths 1884-1900: PRO Kew, FO868/1-2.

Rustchuk (Ruse)
Births 1867-1908, deaths 1867-1903: PRO Kew, FO888/1-2.

Sofia
Births 1934-40: PRO Kew, FO864/1.

Varna
Births 1856-1939, deaths 1851-1929: PRO Kew, FO884/1-5.

BURMA: see INDIA

CANADA

General
All original church registers are held locally in Canada. Some are held by the Public Archives of Canada, 395 Wellington Street, Ottawa K1A 0N3, Canada, but most are in the churches themselves or in local repositories.

Civil registration records do not begin until the 1860s in Nova Scotia and Ontario, and later in the other Canadian provinces. For further details (also for details about Canadian census records, etc.) see *Tracing your Ancestors in Canada* (Public Archives of Canada, 1993).

For records of emigration to Canada see page 12.

For addresses of repositories see page 2

For other sources which may relate to places on this page see 'How to use this guide' (page 1)

Transcripts exist of the following registers:

British Columbia, Mount View
Bur 1892-5: Society of Genealogists.

British Columbia, Osoyoos
Bur 1937-71: Society of Genealogists.

New Brunswick, St John
Mar to 1839: Society of Genealogists.

Newfoundland
For registers held locally in Newfoundland see J. Bishop, 'Newfoundland Family Records' in *Genealogists' Magazine* vol 20 no 9 (1982).

Newfoundland, Twillingate
Bap 1816-23: United Society for the Propagation of the Gospel.

Nova Scotia
Index to births 1864-77: Society of Genealogists.

Nova Scotia, Cape Sable
Index to bap, mar and bur 1799-1841: Leonard H. Smith, *Cape Sable Vital Records . . .* (Clearwater, Florida, c. 1979).

Nova Scotia, Halifax
Bap, mar and bur 1749-68, 1931: Society of Genealogists.

Nova Scotia, St Mary's Bay
Bap and mar 1769-74 and 1799-1801, bur 1801: Leonard H. Smith, *St Mary's Bay . . . Parish Registers* (Clearwater, Florida, 1983).

Nova Scotia, Salmon River
Index to bap, mar and bur 1849-1907: Leonard H. Smith, *Salmon River Vital Records . . .* (Clearwater, Florida, 1977).

Ontario
Presbyterian mar 1800-36: Society of Genealogists.

Ontario, Adolphustown
Presbyterian bap 1782-1839: Society of Genealogists.

For addresses of repositories see page 2

For other sources which may relate to places on this page see 'How to use this guide' (page 1)

Ontario, Ameliasburgh
Presbyterian bap 1801-39: Society of Genealogists.

Ontario, Amherst Isle
Presbyterian bap 1834-40: Society of Genealogists.

Ontario, Brantford
Baptist bap and deaths extracts 1833-84: Society of Genealogists.

Ontario, Camden
Presbyterian bap 1800-39: Society of Genealogists.

Ontario, Cramhe
Presbyterian bap 1799-1820: Society of Genealogists.

Ontario, Ernestown
Bap and mar 1787-1814: Society of Genealogists.
Presbyterian bap 1800-20: Society of Genealogists.

Ontario, Fort Hunter
Indian bap, mar and bur 1735-45: Society of Genealogists.

Ontario, Fredericksburgh
Presbyterian bap 1800-40: Society of Genealogists.

Ontario, Hallowell
Presbyterian bap 1779-1820: Society of Genealogists.
Mar 1803-23: Society of Genealogists.

Ontario, Halton: see *Ontario, Palermo.*

Ontario, Hamilton
Presbyterian bap 1787-1803: Society of Genealogists.
See also *Ontario, Palermo.*

Ontario, Kingston
Bap, mar and bur 1785-1811: printed in A. H. Young, *The Parish Register of Kingston, Upper Canada* (Kingston, 1921) (not available at Guildhall Library).
Bap, mar and bur 1785-1811 (see above): Society of Genealogists.
Presbyterian bap 1802-69, mar 1822-68: Society of Genealogists.

For addresses of repositories see page 2

For other sources which may relate to places on this
page see 'How to use this guide' (page 1)

Ontario, Loughboro
Presbyterian bap 1791-1837: Society of Genealogists.

Ontario, Markham
Methodist bap 1851-66: Society of Genealogists.

Ontario, Marysburgh
Presbyterian bap 1799-1837: Society of Genealogists.

Ontario, Milton: see *Ontario, Palermo.*

Ontario, Murray
Presbyterian bap 1798-1820: Society of Genealogists.

Ontario, Palermo
Methodist bap, mar and bur 1901-56: Society of Genealogists.

Ontario, Pittsburgh
Presbyterian bap 1800-9: Society of Genealogists.

Ontario, Portland
Presbyterian bap 1791-1807: Society of Genealogists.

Ontario, Quinte Bay
Mar 1836-8: Society of Genealogists.

Ontario, Rawdon
Presbyterian bap 1803: Society of Genealogists.

Ontario, Richmond
Presbyterian bap 1811-32: Society of Genealogists.

Ontario, Sheffield
Presbyterian bap 1831-9: Society of Genealogists.

Ontario, Sidney
Presbyterian bap 1800-20: Society of Genealogists.

Ontario, Sophiasburgh
Presbyterian bap 1800-28: Society of Genealogists.

For addresses of repositories see page 2

For other sources which may relate to places on this
page see 'How to use this guide' (page 1)

Ontario, Thurlow
Presbyterian bap 1802-39: Society of Genealogists.

Ontario, Toronto
Bap 1807-1908: Society of Genealogists.

Ontario, Tyendinaga
Presbyterian bap 1826-37: Society of Genealogists.

Prince Edward Island, Charlottetown
Index to bap, mar, bur 1760-1942: Society of Genealogists.
Bap 1777-1803, bur 1805-26: Society of Genealogists.

Quebec
Bap, mar and bur 1790-1882: Society of Genealogists.
Military bap, mar and bur 1797-1815: Society of Genealogists.

Quebec, Dalesville
Baptist bap, mar and bur 1837-43: Society of Genealogists.

Quebec, Levis County
Mar 1820-1948: Society of Genealogists.

Quebec, Montreal
Bap, mar and bur 1706-1980: Society of Genealogists.
Roman Catholic Irish mar 1851-99: Society of Genealogists.

Quebec, Rivière du Loup en Bas
Bap, mar and bur 1841-75: Society of Genealogists.

Quebec, St Charles aux Mines
Index to bap 1717-23: Society of Genealogists.

Quebec, St Joseph
Bap, mar and bur 1835-1950: Society of Genealogists.

Saskatchewan, Mistawasis
Index to Presbyterian (Indian Mission) mar 1905-22: Society of Genealogists.

Saskatchewan, Pleasantville
Index to Presbyterian mar 1903-5: Society of Genealogists.

For addresses of repositories see page 2

For other sources which may relate to places on this
page see 'How to use this guide' (page 1)

Note. Assistance in tracing other church registers may be obtainable from local genealogical societies in Canada, whose addresses can be found in Mary Keysor Meyer (ed.), *Meyer's Directory of Genealogical Societies in the U.S.A. and Canada* (Mount Airy, Maryland, 1990).

CANARY ISLANDS: see SPAIN

CAPE VERDE ISLANDS: see PORTUGAL

CEYLON (SRI LANKA)
Mar 1817 in 'International memoranda' at Guildhall Library: see page 6.

Enquiries about other records (from 1704) should be addressed to the Registrar General's Office, Colombo 1, Sri Lanka.

CHILE
Some entries for bap 1836-90, mar 1836-87 in 'International memoranda' at Guildhall Library: see page 6.

CHINA
Some entries for bap 1872-1907, mar 1864-1911 in 'International memoranda' at Guildhall Library: see page 6.

Amoy (Xiamen)
Births 1850-1950, mar 1850-1949, deaths 1850-1948: PRO Kew, FO663/85-95 and FO681/1.

Bejing: see *Peking*

Canton (Guangzhou)

Births 1864-76, 1944-50, mar 1865-76, 1943-9, deaths 1865-76, 1944-50: PRO Kew, FO681/1-3, 5-9.

Changsha
Births 1905-41, deaths 1906-36: PRO Kew, FO681/10-12.

Chefoo (Yantai)
Births 1861-1943, mar 1872-1940, deaths 1861-1942: PRO Kew, FO681/13-22.

For addresses of repositories see page 2

For other sources which may relate to places on this page see 'How to use this guide' (page 1)

Chekiang (Zhejiang)
Bap 1903-35, mar 1873 and 1903-49: Church Missionary Society.

Chengtu (Chengdu)
Births 1902-15, mar 1904-24, deaths 1904-26: PRO Kew, FO664/3, 5.

Chinanfu (Tsinan)
Births 1906-36, mar 1907-36, deaths 1906-37: PRO Kew, FO681/23-7.

Chinkiang
Births 1865-1926, mar 1865-76, deaths 1865-1927: PRO Kew, FO387/7-11 and FO681/1.

Chunking
Births 1888-1951, mar 1891-1949, deaths 1891-1950: PRO Kew, FO681/28-34.

Dairen (Dalian)
Births 1907-40, mar 1911-40, deaths 1910-40: PRO Kew, FO681/35-7.

Foochow (Fuzhou)
Births 1858-76, 1905-44, mar 1858-76, 1909-42, deaths 1858-76, 1921-45: PRO Kew, FO665/3-8 and FO681/1.

Formosa: see *Taiwan*

Guangzhou: see *Canton*

Hankow (Hankou)
Births 1863-1951, mar 1866-1949, deaths 1861-1950: PRO Kew, FO666/2-22 and FO681/1.

Hong Kong
Deaths 1941-5: PRO Chancery Lane, RG33/11 (index in RG43/14).

Huangpu: see *Whampoa*

Ichang
Births 1879-1938, mar 1881-1937, deaths 1880-1941: PRO Kew, FO667/2-6.

For addresses of repositories see page 2

For other sources which may relate to places on this page see 'How to use this guide' (page 1)

Kaohung: see *Taku*

Kiukiang
Births 1866-1929, mar 1869-1928, deaths 1863-1929: PRO Kew, FO681/1, 39-45.

Kunming (Yunnanfu)
Births 1903-51, mar 1904-49, deaths 1903-50: PRO Kew, FO668/2-3 and FO681/74-5, 77-8.

Kweilin
Births 1942-4, deaths 1943: PRO Kew, FO681/46-7.

Lotu: see Ningpo

Macao
Births, mar and deaths 1819-28: printed in *East India Register* 1821-9.
Bap, mar and bur 1820-33: India Office Library, in N/9/1 (index in Z/N/9/1).
Bap 1820-38, mar 1822-38, bur 1821-38: Guildhall Library, in Ms 11218 (index in Ms 15061/1-2).
Mar 1792 in 'International memoranda' at Guildhall Library: see page 6.
Bur 1818-59 listed in Lindsay Ride, *The Old Protestant Cemetery in Macao* (Hong Kong, 1963).

Mukden (Shenyang)
Births 1949, mar 1947-8, deaths 1949: PRO Kew, FO681/48-9, 79-80.

Nanking (Nanjing)
Births 1930-48, mar 1929-49, deaths 1930-47: PRO Kew, FO681/50-53.

Newchwang
Births, mar and deaths 1869-76: PRO Kew, FO681/1.

Ningpo (Lotu)
Births 1858-76, mar 1849-76, deaths 1856-76: PRO Kew, FO670/2-4 and FO681/1.

Peking (Bejing)
Births 1869-76, 1911-14, deaths 1869-76, 1911-13: PRO Kew, FO564/13-14 and FO681/1.

For addresses of repositories see page 2

For other sources which may relate to places on this page see 'How to use this guide' (page 1)

Shanghai
Bap 1849-1951, mar 1852-1947, bur 1859-99: Lambeth Palace Library, Mss 1564-84.
Births 1856-76, mar and deaths 1851-76: PRO Kew, FO672/1-3 and FO681/1.
Mar 1852-1951: PRO Chancery Lane, RG33/12-32 (index in RG43/7, 9-14).

Shantou: see *Swatow*

Shantung (Shandong)
Bap 1906-50, mar 1912-48, bur 1934-46: Lambeth Palace Library, Mss 1761-4.
Mar 1912-42: PRO Chancery Lane, RG33/33.

Shenyang: see *Mukden*

Sichuan: see *West China diocese*

Swatow (Shantou)
Births 1864-76, 1947-9, mar 1865-76, deaths 1864-76: PRO Kew, FO681/1, 54-6, 81.

Szechwan (Sichuan): see *West China diocese*

Taiwan (Formosa)
Births and mar 1869-76, deaths 1869-1901: PRO Kew, FO681/1 and FO721/1.

Taku (Kaohung)
Births 1862-75, deaths 1871-5: PRO Kew, FO673/9-10.

Tamsui (Tan-shui)
Births, mar, deaths 1866: PRO Kew, FO681/59.

Tengyueh (Teigchung)
Births 1909-41, mar 1913-1941, deaths 1906-41: PRO Kew, FO681/60-62.

Tientsin
Births 1864-1951, mar 1863-1952, deaths 1862-1952: PRO Kew, FO674/297-312, 314-27 and FO681/1.

For addresses of repositories see page 2

For other sources which may relate to places on this
page see 'How to use this guide' (page 1)

Tsinan: see *Chinanfu*

Tsingtao
Births 1911-50, mar 1923-49, deaths 1921-51: PRO Kew, FO673/9-10, FO675/7-8.

Wei-hai-wei (Weihai)
Births, mar and deaths 1899-1930: PRO Chancery Lane, RG33/34 (index in RG43/19).
Births 1899-1941, mar 1905-40, deaths 1900-42: PRO Kew, FO681/63-71.

West China diocese (Szechwan)
Bap 1895-1951: Guildhall Library, Ms 17360 (transcript 1895-1907, Ms 11218C; bap 1895-1907 also entered and indexed in 'International memoranda', for which see page 6).
Mar 1888-1948: Guildhall Library, Ms 17361 (mar 1889-1911 also entered and indexed in 'International memoranda', for which see page 6).
Mar 1894-1950: Guildhall Library, Mss 11218A-B (mar 1894-1911 also entered and indexed in 'International memoranda', for which see page 6; index to mar 1912-1950 in Ms 15061/1-2, under 'China').

Whampoa
Births 1865-76, mar 1869-76, deaths 1865-76: PRO Kew, FO681/1, 72-3.
Bur 1820-24: Guildhall Library, in Ms 11218 (index in Ms 15061/1-2).
Bur 1820-34: India Office Library, in N/9/1 (index in Z/N/9/1).

Xiamen: see *Amoy*

Yantai: see *Chefoo*

Yunnanfu: see *Kunming*

Zhejiang: see *Chekiang*

COLOMBIA
Some entries for bap 1851, mar 1839-82 in 'International memoranda' at Guildhall Library: see page 6.
Mar 1824-7: PRO Chancery Lane, in RG33/155 (index in RG43/7).

Cartagena
Births 1853-1924, deaths 1858-1927: PRO Kew, FO736/2-3.

For addresses of repositories see page 2

For other sources which may relate to places on this
page see 'How to use this guide' (page 1)

Santa Marta
Births 1862-1916, deaths 1862-1923: PRO Kew, FO736/7.

CORFU: see GREECE

CORSICA: see FRANCE

CUBA: see WEST INDIES

CURAÇAO
Portuguese Jewish births and mar 1743-1831: Society of Genealogists.
Births 1897-1969, mar 1922-9, deaths 1889-1965: PRO Kew, in FO907/1-11, 23-6, 32, 36-7.

CYPRUS
Bap 1939-52: Society of Genealogists.

DENMARK
General
Some entries for bap 1816-33, mar 1826-89 in 'International memoranda' at Guildhall Library: see page 6.
Many entries in 'Miscellaneous' series 1826-1951 at PRO Chancery Lane (see page 9); the series also includes separate death registers for Denmark and its colonies 1842-72 (RG35/4-7).

Copenhagen
Bap, mar and bur 1835-99 are indexed in A. K. Higgins, *An index to the baptisms, marriages and burials registered by the chaplains to the British legation in Copenhagen, 1835-1899, comprising from 1887 the registers of St Alban's Church, Copenhagen, with a list of . . . inscriptions in St Alban's Church* (Copenhagen, 1989).
Bap, mar and bur 1835-99 (see above): Society of Genealogists.
Bap 1836-65, mar 1835-65, bur 1836-65: Guildhall Library, Ms 11212 (index in Ms 15061/1-2).
Mar 1853-70: PRO Kew, FO211/236.
Mar 1853-74: PRO Chancery Lane, RG33/35 (index in RG43/7).

Elsinore
Bap 1833-8, bur 1833-9: Guildhall Library, Ms 11213 (index, 1833-5 only, in Ms 15061/1-2).

For addresses of repositories see page 2

For other sources which may relate to places on this page see 'How to use this guide' (page 1)

DOMINICA: see **WEST INDIES**

DOMINICAN REPUBLIC: see **WEST INDIES**

DUTCH EAST INDIES: see **INDONESIA**

DUTCH GUIANA: see **SURINAM**

ECUADOR
Guayaquil
Deaths 1886-7: PRO Kew, FO521/2.

EGYPT
Alexandria
Military bap, mar and bur 1801: Society of Genealogists.
Bap, mar and bur 1841-59: Guildhall Library, Ms 11215 (index in Ms 15061/1-2).
Church of Scotland bap 1858-1957, mar 1860-1954: National Library of Scotland, Acc 7548/G8-9, 11-12.
Mar 1842 in 'International memoranda' at Guildhall Library: see page 6.

Cairo
Church of Scotland bap 1899-1959, mar 1910-56: National Library of Scotland, Acc 7548/G56-7.

ESTONIA: see **RUSSIA**

FALKLAND ISLANDS
Port Stanley
Bap 1840-1949, mar 1844-1949, bur 1838-1949: Society of Genealogists.

South Georgia
Births, mar and deaths 1910-48: Society of Genealogists.

FINLAND
Abo: see *Turku*

Brahestad: see *Raahe*

For addresses of repositories see page 2

For other sources which may relate to places on this page see 'How to use this guide' (page 1)

Helsinki
Births 1914-24, deaths 1924: PRO Kew, FO753/19 and FO768/5.
Bap 1920-47, mar 1921-61, banns 1926-50, bur 1921-38, cremations 1933-49: Guildhall Library, Ms 20892. Transcript of bap 1920-39 (incomplete), mar 1921-4 and 1926-39, bur 1921-38, cremations 1933-9: Ms 11214, indexed in Ms 15061/1-2. Duplicate register of bap 1946, mar 1941 and 1949-51: Ms 20892A.

Kristinestad
Deaths 1928: PRO Kew, FO756/1.

Raahe (Brahestad)
Deaths 1930: PRO Kew, FO755/1.

Tampere (Tammerfors)
Births 1906-23, deaths 1909-34: PRO Kew, FO769/1-2.

Turku (Abo)
Births 1928, deaths 1929: PRO Kew, FO754/1-2.

Vyborg: see **RUSSIA**

FORMOSA: see CHINA, *Taiwan*

FRANCE
General
Some entries for bap 1817-1916, mar 1816-90, bur 1817-22 in 'International memoranda' at Guildhall Library: see page 6.
Many entries in 'Miscellaneous' series 1826-1951 at PRO Chancery Lane (see page 9); the series also includes separate death registers for France and its colonies 1831-71 (RG35/8-16) and for France 1914-21 (military deaths only; incomplete) (RG35/45-57).
Some entries for bap post 1920 in the Bishop of Gilbraltar's memorandum book at Guildhall Library: see page 6.

Aix les Bains
Bap 1886-1933, mar 1921-7, bur 1885-1938: Guildhall Library, Ms 14593.

Arras
Bap 1972-5: Guildhall Library, in Ms 21477.

For addresses of repositories see page 2

For other sources which may relate to places on this page see 'How to use this guide' (page 1)

Avranches
Bap 1821-8: Guildhall Library, in Ms 10891B (index in Ms 15061/1- 2).
Bap 1828-1905, mar 1867-94, bur 1829-1908: United Society for the Propagation of the Gospel.
Bap and bur 1864-73: Guildhall Library, in Ms 11222 (index in Ms 15061/1-2).

Beaulieu-sur-Mer
Bap, mar, bur 1906-date: Beaulieu-sur-Mer Anglican Chaplaincy, details available from Guildhall Library.

Biarritz
Bap 1862-80, bur 1874-80: Guildhall Library, in Ms 11222 (index in Ms 15061/1-2).
Bur 1963-9: Guildhall Library, in Ms 15703A.

Bordeaux
Bap, mar and bur 1611-1792: Society of Genealogists.

Boulogne
Bap 1815-96, mar 1829-95, bur 1815-96: PRO Chancery Lane, RG33/37- 48 (index in RG33/161; also index to bap in RG43/1, mar in RG43/7, bur in RG43/3).
Bap 1817-46, mar 1833-46, bur 1815-46: Guildhall Library, Ms 10891A (index in Ms 15061/1-2).
Bap, mar and bur 1847-1901: British Library, Add Ms 36992.
Mar 1897-1940: Guildhall Library, Ms 21023.
Mar 1906-24: Guildhall Library, Ms 21024.
Bur 1972-3: Guildhall Library, in Ms 21477. Bur 1972 also in Ms 16944.

Brest
Births 1842: PRO Chancery Lane, in RG33/155 (index in RG43/1).

Caen
Bap, mar and bur 1560-70: Society of Genealogists.

Calais
Bap 1817-78, mar 1818-72, bur 1819-78: PRO Chancery Lane, RG33/50-5 (index in RG33/49).
Bap 1903-49: Guildhall Library, Ms 23610.

For addresses of repositories see page 2

For other sources which may relate to places on this page see 'How to use this guide' (page 1)

Bur 1858-1904: Guildhall Library, Ms 21025.
Bur 1972: Guildhall Library, in Ms 16944.

Cannes
Bap and bur 1860-1933: Guildhall Library, Ms 23611.
Bap, mar and bur 1870-9: Guildhall Library, Ms 20987.
Bap 1887-1960: Guildhall Library, Ms 23616.
Mar 1903-28: Guildhall Library, Ms 23612.

Cap d'Antibes
Bap 1926-56: Guildhall Library, Ms 23619.
Bur 1926-63: Guildhall Library, Ms 23620.

Chantilly
Bap 1854-72, mar 1869-72, bur 1854-72: Guildhall Library, Ms 29395.
Bap 1872-1922: Guildhall Library, Ms 22940/1.
Bap 1923-51: Guildhall Library, Ms 22940/2.
Bap 1944-53, mar 1944-57, bur 1944-56: Guildhall Library, Ms 29396/1.
Bap 1958-72, mar 1960-72, bur 1957-73: Guildhall Library, Ms 22943.
Mar 1872-1940: Guildhall Library, Ms 22941.
Bur 1872-1940: Guildhall Library, Ms 22942.
Bur 1956-7: Guildhall Library, Ms 29396/2.

Compiègne
Bap 1868-1914, mar 1869-1907: Chantilly Anglican Chaplaincy, details available from Guildhall Library.

Corsica
Death 1879: Guildhall Library, in Ms 20996.

Dieppe
Bap 1825-9, bur 1825-8: Guildhall Library, in Ms 10891B (index in Ms 15061/1-2).
Births 1872-92, deaths 1871-94: PRO Kew, FO712/1-3.

Givet
Births, mar and bur 1803-12: Society of Genealogists.

La Rochelle
Bur 1831-5: Guildhall Library, in Ms 11818.

For addresses of repositories see page 2

For other sources which may relate to places on this page see 'How to use this guide' (page 1)

Le Havre
Bap, mar and bur 1817-63: PRO Chancery Lane, RG33/56-7 (index to bap in RG43/1, mar in RG43/7, bur in RG43/3).

Le Touquet
Bap 1968 and 1971: Guildhall Library, in Ms 16944.
Mar 1938: Guildhall Library, in Ms 21023.

Le Tréport
Births 1917-26, deaths 1899-1929: PRO Kew, FO713/1-2.

Lille
Bap 1859-63: Guildhall Library, in Ms 11222 (index in Ms 15061/1-2).

Loudun
Bap 1566-77, mar 1566-82: Society of Genealogists.

Lyons
Bap 1854-1967: Guildhall Library, in Ms 14533.
Mar 1868-1969: Guildhall Library, Ms 14534.
Banns 1878-1911: Guildhall Library, Ms 14535.
Bur 1863-1961: Guildhall Library, Ms 14536.

Monaco
Bap 1892-50, mar 1925-51, bur 1893-1950: Society of Genealogists.
Bap 1892-date, mar 1925-date, bur 1893-date: Monte Carlo Anglican Chaplaincy, details available from Guildhall Library.

Nantes
Bap 1867-79: Guildhall Library, Ms 11222B.
Mar 1851-67: PRO Kew, FO384/1.

Nice
Bap 1823-38, mar 1826-38, bur 1822-38: Guildhall Library, in Ms 11222 (index in Ms 15061/1-2).
Bap and bur 1868-84: Guildhall Library, Ms 20988.

Paris
Bap and mar 1718, 1720: Lambeth Palace Library, Ms 1552B.
Bap 1784-9 and 1801-69, mar 1784-9 and 1801-90, bur 1784-9 and 1801-69: PRO Chancery Lane, RG33/58-77 (index to bap in RG43/1, mar in RG43/7, bur in RG43/3).

For addresses of repositories see page 2

For other sources which may relate to places on this
page see 'How to use this guide' (page 1)

Bap 1816-28, mar 1816-45, bur 1815-28: Guildhall Library, Ms 10891 (index at front of Ms 10891 and in Ms 15061/1-2).

Bap 1830-2 and 1835-9, bur 1830-9: Guildhall Library, in Ms 10891B (index in Ms 15061/1-2, bap 1830-2 and bur 1830-5 under 'Germains', bap 1835-9 and bur 1836-9 under 'Paris').

Mar licence certificates and allegations 1828-9 and 1835-7: Guildhall Library, Ms 10891C.

Mar 1935-7: PRO Kew, FO630/1.

Pau

Bap 1842-4 and 1866-78, mar 1843-4 and 1868-77, bur 1865-78: Guildhall Library, in Ms 11222 (index to bap, mar and bur, to 1875 only, in Ms 15061/1-2).

Rennes

Mar 1826: Guildhall Library, in Ms 10891B (index in Ms 15061/1-2).

Rouen

Bap 1843-4: PRO Chancery Lane, RG33/78 (index in RG43/1).

Bap 1852-9: see *Sotteville-les-Rouen.*

St Germain-en-Laye

Jacobite bap, mar, bur extracts 1689-1720: Society of Genealogists.

St Malo

Bap 1838-42, bur 1838-9: Guildhall Library, in Ms 10891B (index in Ms 15061/1-2, under 'Malo').

St Omer

Bap 1817-47: PRO Chancery Lane, in RG33/50 (index in RG33/49).

Mar 1919: Guildhall Library, in Ms 21023.

St Servan

Bap and bur 1824-44: Guildhall Library, in Ms 10891B (index in Ms 15061/1-2).

Bap 1848-82, bur 1848-79: Guildhall Library, Ms 11222A/1 (index in Ms 15061/1-2).

Bap 1883-96, mar 1884-95, bur 1884-96: Guildhall Library, Ms 11222A/2 (index in Ms 15061/1-2).

For addresses of repositories see page 2

For other sources which may relate to places on this page see 'How to use this guide' (page 1)

Sotteville-les-Rouen
Bap 1852-9: Guildhall Library, in Ms 11222 (index in Ms 15061/1-2).

Tamaris-sur-Mer
Bap 1928-70: Guildhall Library, Ms 23623.
Bur 1926-30: Guildhall Library, in Ms 23624.

Tours
Bur 1841-3: Guildhall Library, in Ms 11818.

Verdun-sur-Meuse
Births, mar and bur 1803-12: Society of Genealogists.
Bap 1804-14, mar and bur 1806-14 (extracts): Society of Genealogists.

Versailles
Bap 1814-1973, mar 1822-1979, bur 1814-1974: Versailles Anglican Chaplaincy, details available from Guildhall Library.

GERMANY

General
Some entries for bap 1819-91, mar 1817-91, deaths and bur 1858-92 in 'International memoranda' at Guildhall Library: see page 6.
Bap of civilians in chaplaincies of the British Army on the Rhine 1949-56: Guildhall Library, Ms 11225 (index in Ms 15061/1-2, under 'Germany').
Bap of civilians in chaplaincies of the British Army on the Rhine 1954-61: Guildhall Library, Ms 11225A (index in Ms 15061/1-2, under 'Germany').
Bap of civilians in chaplaincies of the British Army on the Rhine 1969-76: Guildhall Library, Ms 11225B.

Aachen (Aix la Chapelle)
Bap 1876-1918, mar 1919, bur 1898-1912: United Society for the Propagation of the Gospel.
Deaths 1925: PRO Kew, FO604/7.

Baden-Baden
Bap 1833-1928, mar 1838-1911, bur 1834-1923: United Society for the Propagation of the Gospel.
Bap 1833-92, mar 1838-90, bur 1834-91: Guildhall Library, Ms 11203 (index in Ms 15061/1-2).
Bap 1893-1912, mar 1894-1908, bur 1892-1908: Guildhall Library, Ms 11203A (index in Ms 15061/1-2).

For addresses of repositories see page 2

For other sources which may relate to places on this page see 'How to use this guide' (page 1)

Bavaria
Bap 1860-1, mar 1860-1 and 1884-97, deaths 1860-1: PRO Kew, FO149/99 and FO151/3.

Berlin
Births 1944-54, deaths 1944-5: PRO Kew, FO601/2-6.

Bonn
Bap 1859-73, mar 1860 and 1873, bur 1859-73: Guildhall Library, Ms 11206 (index in Ms 15061/1-2).

Bremen
Births 1872-1914, mar 1893-1908: PRO Kew, FO585/1,5.

Bremerhaven
Births 1872-1914: PRO Kew, FO585/1.

Breslau: see **POLAND**

Cologne
Births and mar 1850-66, deaths 1850-66 and 1879-81: PRO Kew, FO155/5-8, 11, 17.

Danzig: see **POLAND**

Darmstadt
Births 1869-98, deaths 1871-1905: PRO Kew, FO716/1-2.

Dresden
Births, bap and bur 1817-36: PRO Chancery Lane, RG33/79 (index to births and bap in RG43/1, bur in RG43/3).
Bap 1837-49, mar 1898, bur 1837-48: Guildhall Library, Ms 11205 (index to bap and bur in Ms 15061/1-2).
Births and deaths 1859-66: PRO Chancery Lane, RG33/80 (index to births in RG43/1, deaths in RG43/3).
Births 1901-14, mar 1899-1900: PRO Kew, FO292/2-5.

Düsseldorf
Bap and bur 1861-77: Guildhall Library, Ms 11204 (index to bap and bur 1861-8 in Ms 15061/1-2).
Births 1873-84 and 1922-7, mar 1873-8, 1893-8 and 1920-34, deaths 1876-84 and 1925: PRO Kew, FO604/1-9, 11.

For addresses of repositories see page 2

For other sources which may relate to places on this
page see 'How to use this guide' (page 1)

Essen
Births 1922-7: PRO Kew, FO604/11.

Frankfurt am Main
Mar 1836-65: PRO Kew, FO208/90.

Freiburg im Breisgau
Bap 1863-1914, mar 1903-6, bur 1863-1913: United Society for the Propagation of the Gospel.

Hamburg, Church of the English Merchant Adventurers residing in Hamburg
Bap and mar 1617-1807: Staatsarchiv of Hamburg, ABC-Strasse 19, Eingang A, 20354, Hamburg, Germany.
Bur registers were not kept by the English Church. 17th and 18th century bur can be found in the records of other churches held by the Staatsarchiv of Hamburg. Bur 1665-1716, recorded in the registers of the Dutch Reformed Church at Altona, are printed in *Genealogists' Magazine* vol 10 no 14 (1950).

Hamburg, Anglican Chaplaincy
Bap 1815-67, mar and bur 1834-65: Staatsarchiv of Hamburg, ABC-Strasse 19, Eingang A, 20354, Hamburg, Germany.
Bap 1815-17, 1820-1930: Guildhall Library, Ms 25100-1.
Bap and mar 1820-38, bur 1821-38: Guildhall Library, Ms 11201 (index in Ms 15061/1-2.
Births, bap and mar certificates, 1836-1907: Guildhall Library, Ms 25104.
Mar 1816-17: Guildhall Library, Ms 25100.
Mar 1820-1939: Guildhall Library, Ms 25102/1-2.
Bur 1821-1914: Guildhall Library, Ms 25103/1-2.

Hamburg, English Reformed Church
Bap 1818-65, mar 1819-65, bur 1818-65: Staatsarchiv of Hamburg, ABC-Strasse 19, Eingang A, 20354, Hamburg, Germany.
Bap 1818-1938: Guildhall Library, Ms 25109/1-3 and Ms 25110 (indexed 1818-1909 in Ms 25109/2).
Birth certificates 1830-67: Guildhall Library, Ms 25109A.
Births 1861-72: Guildhall Library, Ms 25111.
Mar 1819-31: Guildhall Library, Ms 25112.
Mar certificates 1860-1934: Guildhall Library, Ms 25112A.
Bur 1818-67: Guildhall Library, Ms 25113.
Bur certificates 1838-66: Guildhall Library, Ms 25113A.

For addresses of repositories see page 2

For other sources which may relate to places on this page see 'How to use this guide' (page 1)

Hanover
Bap, mar, deaths and bur 1839-59: PRO Chancery Lane, RG33/81 (index to bap in RG43/1, mar in RG43/7, deaths and bur in RG43/3).
Births 1861-6: PRO Kew, FO717/1.

Heidelberg
Bap 1869-1914, mar 1889: United Society for the Propagation of the Gospel.

Karlsruhe
Births 1860-4, deaths 1859-64: PRO Kew, FO718/1-2.

Konigsberg: see **RUSSIA**

Leipzig
Bap 1864-76, mar 1865-75, banns 1867-75, bur 1866-76: Guildhall Library, Ms 11205A (index in Ms 15061/1-2).
Mar 1850-65, deaths 1850-69: PRO Kew, FO299/22.

Munich
Bap 1862-7: Guildhall Library, Ms 11207 (index in Ms 15061/1-2).

Nuremburg
Bur 1517-72: Society of Genealogists.

Silesia: see **POLAND**

Stettin: see **POLAND**

Wiesbaden
Bap 1848-67, mar 1865-6, bur 1848-66: Guildhall Library, Ms 11202/1 (index in Ms 15061/1-2).
Bap 1868-76, mar 1871-6, bur 1867-76: Guildhall Library, Ms 11202/2 (index in Ms 15061/1-2).

GIBRALTAR
Military bap and mar 1807-12, bur 1807: Guildhall Library, Ms 10446D (index in Ms 15061/1-2).
Military mar 1810 in 'International memoranda' at Guildhall Library: see page 6.
Mar allegations 1859-73: Guildhall Library, Ms 20979.
Other registers (civilian from 1696, military from 1769) are held locally in

---

For addresses of repositories see page 2

For other sources which may relate to places on this page see 'How to use this guide' (page 1)

Gibraltar. See L. R. Burness, 'Genealogical Research in Gibraltar', i.
Genealogists' Magazine vol 21 no 1 (1983). Guildhall Library has details of
registers (bap, mar, bur 1836-date) held at the Cathedral of the Holy Trinity,
Gibraltar.

GEORGIA
Batum and *Poti:* see **RUSSIA**

GREECE
General
Some entries for bap 1827-93, mar 1829-90 in 'International memoranda' at
Guildhall Library: see page 6.
Some entries for bap post 1920 in the Bishop of Gibraltar's memorandum
book at Guildhall Library: see page 6.

Athens
Bap 1834-91, mar 1840-1945, bur 1840-1941: Society of Genealogists.
Bap 1834-97, mar 1840-1924, bur 1835-97: Guildhall Library, Ms 23838
(index to bap 1834-98, mar and bur 1840-98 in Ms 23842/1).
Bap and bur 1898-1934: Guildhall Library, Ms 23839 (index 1898-1908 in
Ms 23842/2).
Mar 1924-38: Guildhall Library, Ms 23840.

Corfu
Bap 1865-1974, mar 1866-1946: Society of Genealogists.

Ionian Islands
Births, bap and mar 1818-64, deaths and bur 1836-64: Office of Population
Censuses and Surveys (index at PRO Chancery Lane, births and bap in
RG43/1, mar in RG43/7, deaths and bur in RG43/3).
Bap, mar, deaths and bur 1849-59: PRO Chancery Lane, RG33/82 (index to
bap in RG43/1, mar in RG43/7, deaths and bur in RG43/3).
Bap 1874: Guildhall Library, in Ms 20996.

GRENADA: see WEST INDIES

GUADELOUPE: see WEST INDIES

GUATEMALA
Mar 1863 in 'International memoranda' at Guildhall Library: see page 6.

For addresses of repositories see page 2

For other sources which may relate to places on this
page see 'How to use this guide' (page 1)

NA: see **BRITISH GUIANA**

see **WEST INDIES**

II

Honolulu
Births 1848-93: PRO Kew, FO331/59.
Mar 1850-3: PRO Chancery Lane, RG33/155 (index in RG43/7).

HOLLAND: see NETHERLANDS

HONG KONG: see CHINA

HUNGARY

Budapest
Mar 1875-99: PRO Kew, FO114/5.

INDIA

General
Bap, mar and bur, apparently complete for all India 1698-1948, and incomplete 1949-68: India Office Library, N/1-5 and N/10-11 (indexes in Z/N/1-5 and Z/N/10-11). These records include bap, mar and bur for former parts of India which are now Burma, Pakistan and Bangladesh. For details of other biographical material at the India Office Library, see I. A. Baxter, *India Office Library and Records: A Brief Guide to Biographical Sources* (London, 1990).

A number of abstracts of vital events in India from various sources are held at the Society of Genealogists. Sources at the Society of Genealogists are described in Neville C. Taylor, *Sources of Anglo-Indian Genealogy in the Library of the Society of Genealogists* (London, c.1990).
Registers or transcripts for the following localities are available at repositories other than the India Office Library, and/or in published form:

Amritsar
Bap 1878-1946, mar 1853-1944: Society of Genealogists.

For addresses of repositories see page 2

For other sources which may relate to places on this
page see 'How to use this guide' (page 1)

Assam
Church of Scotland bap, mar and bur 1939-59: Scottish Record Office,
CH2/1148/4-6.

Benares
Bap 1810-54, mar 1810-40, bur 1810-55: Society of Genealogists.

Bengal
Bap 1713-88, mar 1713-92, bur 1713-88: Society of Genealogists.
Births, mar and deaths 1807-43: printed in *East India Register* 1809-44.
Births, mar and deaths 1813-62: printed in *Bengal Directory* 1814-63 (only
1826 available at Guildhall Library).
Mar 1821 in 'International memoranda' at Guildhall Library: see page 6.

Bikaner: see *Indian Native States*

Bombay
Births, mar and deaths 1805-81: printed in *Bombay Directory* 1806-82 (not
available at Guildhall Library).
Births, mar and deaths 1807-43: printed in *East India Register* 1809-44.
Bap 1818: Guildhall Library, in Ms 11219 (index in Ms 15061/1-2).

Burma
Bur 1826-1980: Society of Genealogists.

Burma, Rangoon
Mar 1929-42: PRO Chancery Lane, RG33/10 (index in RG43/11-13).

Calcutta
Bap 1732-1908, mar 1723-1859, bur 1757-1813 (extracts): Society of
Genealogists.
Baptist bap extracts 1800-1908: Society of Genealogists.
Mar 1759-79: Society of Genealogists.

Canwar
Mar extracts 1863-1917: Society of Genealogists.

Cochin
Dutch Reformed mar extracts 1751-1801: Society of Genealogists.

Coorg
Bur 1892-1962: Society of Genealogists.

For addresses of repositories see page 2

For other sources which may relate to places on this
page see 'How to use this guide' (page 1)

Dalhousie
Bap 1862-1935, mar 1865-1942, bur 1860-1932: Society of Genealogists.

Deccan States: see *Kolhapur and Deccan States*

Delhi
Church of Scotland bap 1876-1929, bur 1887-1913 (extracts): Society of Genealogists.
Roman Catholic bap 1900, mar 1861-1922, bur 1860-1932 (extracts): Society of Genealogists.

Fatehgarh Camp
Mar and deaths 1777-1857: Society of Genealogists.

Fort St George: see *Madras*

Gulmarg
Bap and mar 1896-1941: Society of Genealogists.

Gurdaspur
Births 1902-41, bap 1870-1930: Society of Genealogists.
Mar 1871-1945, bur 1868-1944 (extracts): Society of Genealogists.

Gwalior: see *Indian Native States*

Hyderabad: see *Indian Native States*

Indian Native States
Births and deaths 1894-1947: PRO Chancery Lane, RG33/90-113 (index in RG43/15).

Jaipur: see *Indian Native States*

Jammu and Kashmir
Births 1917-47: PRO Chancery Lane, RG33/157.

Jhansi
Bap 1841-62, mar 1888-1928 (extracts): Society of Genealogists.

For addresses of repositories see page 2

For other sources which may relate to places on this page see 'How to use this guide' (page 1)

Jutogh
Bur 1888-1945: Society of Genealogists.

Kalka
Bap 1901-43, mar 1921-42, bur 1883-1943: Society of Genealogists.

Kasauli
Bap 1845-1919, mar 1857-1919, bur 1843-1945 (extracts): Society of Genealogists.

Kashmir: see *Jammu and Kashmir*

Kolhapur and Deccan States
Births 1930-46: PRO Chancery Lane, RG33/158.

Madras
Births, mar and deaths 1805-1903: printed in *Madras Almanac* 1806-1904 (only 1806 available at Guildhall Library).
Births, mar and deaths 1807-43: printed in *East India Register* 1809-44.
Church of Scotland bap 1842-1929: Society of Genealogists.
Mar 1680-1815: printed in *Marriages at Fort St George, Madras,* 1680-1815 (anon.; Exeter, 1907) (not available at Guildhall Library); also in *The Genealogist,* New series, vol 19-23 (1903-7).
Bur 1680-1900: printed in C. H. Malden, *Burials at St Mary's, Madras, 1680-1900* (Madras, 1903-5) (not available at Guildhall Library).
Mar 1680-1800, bur 1680-1900 (see above): Society of Genealogists.

Madras States: see Indian Native States

Meerut
Deaths and bur 1815-75, bur extracts 1857: Society of Genealogists.

Mysore: see *Indian Native States*

Ootacamund
Mar 1831-66: Society of Genealogists.

Punjab States: see *Indian Native States*

Rajputana (Eastern): see *Indian Native States*

For addresses of repositories see page 2

For other sources which may relate to places on this page see 'How to use this guide' (page 1)

Rangoon: see *Burma*

Simla
Bap 1838-1914, mar 1838-1944, bur 1838-1945 (extracts): Society of Genealogists.
Roman Catholic bap 1867-1923, mar 1881-1942, bur 1863-1943 (extracts): Society of Genealogists.
See also: *Jutogh*

Srinagar
Bap 1863-1941, mar 1876-1941, bur 1849-1941: Society of Genealogists.
Deaths 1926-47: PRO Chancery Lane, RG33/159.

Tranquebar
Danish mar 1767-1845: Society of Genealogists.

Travancore: see *Indian Native States*

Trichinopoly
Bap 1751-1847, mar 1767-91 and 1805-42: United Society for the Propagation of the Gospel.

Trivandrum: see *Indian Native States*

Udaipur
Births 1938-47: PRO Chancery Lane, RG33/160.

INDONESIA (DUTCH EAST INDIES)
General
Many entries among registrations for the Netherlands and its colonies in 'Miscellaneous' series 1826-1951 at PRO Chancery Lane (see page 9).

Borneo, Balikpapan
Births 1907, deaths 1897-1907: PRO Kew, FO221/2-3.

Java, Semarang
Births 1869-1941, deaths 1874-98 and 1912-40: PRO Kew, FO803/1-2.

New Guinea: see **NEW GUINEA**

Sumatra, Bencoolen
Bur 1777-1858: Society of Genealogists.

For addresses of repositories see page 2

For other sources which may relate to places on this page see 'How to use this guide' (page 1)

Sumatra, Fort Marlborough
Bap, mar and bur 1759-1825: India Office Library, N/7/1 (index in Z/N/ 7/1).
Births, mar and deaths 1818-23: printed in *East India Register* 1819-25.

Sumatra, Oleh Leh (Ule Lue)
Births and deaths 1883-4: PRO Kew, FO220/12.

IONIAN ISLANDS: see GREECE

IRAN (PERSIA)
Abadan
Mar 1913 in 'International memoranda' at Guildhall Library: see page 6.

Birjand
Births 1829-1931: PRO Kew, FO923/1.

Bushire (Bushehr)
Births 1849-1947, mar and deaths 1849-95: PRO Kew, FO560/1-2.

Hamadan
Births 1918-30, mar 1914-32, deaths 1917-29: PRO Kew, FO923/3.

Isfahan (Esfahan)
Births 1892-1950, mar 1893-1951, deaths 1892-1945: PRO Kew, FO799/34-7.

Julfa (Jolfa)
Bap 1870-9, mar 1877, bur 1873 in 'International memoranda' at Guildhall Library: see page 6. Bap 1875-8 and mar 1877 also in Ms 11215A.

Kain: see *Sistan and Kain*

Kashvin: see *Qazvin*

Kerman
Births 1903-45, mar 1905-37, deaths 1898-1946: PRO Kew, FO923/6-8.

Kermanshahan
Births 1919-49, mar 1906-47, deaths 1920-47: PRO Kew, FO923/9-12.

Mashhad (Meshed)
Births 1905-38, mar 1895-1949, deaths 1899-1950: PRO Kew, FO923/13-17.

For addresses of repositories see page 2

For other sources which may relate to places on this
page see 'How to use this guide' (page 1)

Qazvin (Kashvin)
Births 1917-20: PRO Kew, FO923/5.

Resht (Rasht)
Births 1948, mar 1950: PRO Kew, FO923/18-19.

Sistan and Kain (Zahedan)
Births 1904-50, mar 1931-8, deaths 1889-1932: PRO Kew, FO923/20-25.

Tabriz
Bap 1844 in 'International memoranda' at Guildhall Library: see page 6.
Births 1851-1951, mar 1850-1903, deaths 1882-1944: PRO Kew, FO451/2-8.

Tehran
Bur 1811-1969: Society of Genealogists.

Zahedan: see *Sistan and Kain*

IRAQ (MESOPOTAMIA)
General
Births 1915-31, bap 1915-24, mar and deaths 1915-31: PRO Chancery Lane, RG33/133-7 (index in RG33/138-9 and RG43/16).
Bap 1916-22, mar 1917-28: Lambeth Palace Library, Mss 2669 and 2672.

Baghdad
Bap 1883-1967, mar 1922-46, bur 1922-41: Lambeth Palace Library, Mss 2669-70, 2673 and 2676.

Basrah
Bap 1943-56, mar 1943-66, bur 1943-53: Lambeth Palace Library, Mss 2505, 2507 and 2675.
Mar 1922-8: Guildhall Library, Ms 11221 (index in Ms 15061/1-2).

Kirkuk
Bap 1947-72, mar 1947-57: Lambeth Palace Library, Mss 2671 and 2674.

ISRAEL: see PALESTINE

ITALY
General
Some entries for bap 1818-93, mar 1814-90, bur 1856-85 in 'International memoranda' at Guildhall Library: see page 6.

For addresses of repositories see page 2

For other sources which may relate to places on this page see 'How to use this guide' (page 1)

Some entries for bap post 1920 in the Bishop of Gibraltar's memorandum book at Guildhall Library: see page 6.

Agrigento (Girgenti)
Births 1857-1904, deaths 1857-85: PRO Kew, FO653/2-4.

Alassio
Bap 1881-1937, mar 1882-1932, bur 1881-1946: Guildhall Library, in Ms 23626.

Bagni di Lucca
Bap 1853-1944: Guildhall Library, Ms 22927.
Mar 1887-1901: Guildhall Library, in Ms 22914.
Bur 1842-1953: Guildhall Library, Ms 22910.

Bologna
Bap, mar and bur 1887-1900: Guildhall Library, in Ms 23772/1.
Bap, mar and bur 1900-25: Guildhall Library, in Ms 23772/2.
Mar 1932: Guildhall Library, in Ms 23776.

Bordighera
Bap 1882-1961: Guildhall Library, Ms 22395.
Mar 1927-34: Guildhall Library, Ms 22396.

Carrara
Bur 1876-1928: Guildhall Library, Ms 23783.

Catania
Births 1878-1939, deaths 1878-1940: PRO Kew, FO653/5-7.

Florence
Births 1816-52, mar 1816-56: PRO Kew, FO170/6 and FO352/43c.
Bap, mar and bur 1833-9: Guildhall Library, Ms 23773. Also entered in Ms 20989/1 and 23774. Bap 1835-6 also entered in Ms 11208 (and indexed in Ms 15061/1-2, under 'Rome').
Bap 1840-50, mar 1840-54, bur 1840-51: Guildhall Library, Ms 23774. Also entered in Ms 20989/1-2.
Bap 1851-45: Guildhall Library, Ms 23775. Some entries to 1899 also recorded in Ms 20989/2.
Mar 1840-55 and 1865-71: PRO Chancery Lane, RG33/114-15 (index in RG43/7). Mar 1865-71 also entered in Guildhall Library, Ms 23781. Some entries also recorded in Ms 20989/2.

For addresses of repositories see page 2

For other sources which may relate to places on this page see 'How to use this guide' (page 1)

Mar 1854-1944: Guildhall Library, Ms 23776. Some entries to 1869 also recorded in Ms 20989/2.
Bur 1851-1912: Guildhall Library, Ms 23777/1. Some entries to 1869 also recorded in Ms 20989/2.
Bur 1912-39: Guildhall Library, Ms 23777/2.

Gela (Terranova)
Births 1904-30: PRO Kew, FO653/8.

Genoa
Bap 1824-49, mar 1825-49, bur 1824-49: Guildhall Library, Ms 11210 (index in Ms 15061/1-2).

Girgenti: see *Agrigento*

Leghorn
Births 1784-1824, bap, mar and bur 1707-1824: PRO Chancery Lane, RG33/116-17 (index to bap in RG43/1, mar in RG43/7, bur in RG43/3). Bap 1709-83 mar 1708-80, bur 1714-83 also entered in Guildhall Library, Ms 23782 (indexed).
Bap 1825-51, mar 1826-50, bur 1825-51: Guildhall Library, Ms 20990. Bap 1832-7, mar 1832-5 and bur 1832-7 also entered in Ms 11211 (and indexed in Ms 15061/1-2).
Mar 1823: Guildhall Library, in Ms 11211 (index in Ms 15061/1-2).

Licata
Births 1871-1900, deaths 1871-1890: PRO Kew, FO720/1.

Marsala
Births and deaths 1847-1922: PRO Kew, FO653/9-11.

Massa
Bur 1882 and 1904: Guildhall Library, in Ms 23783.

Mazzara (Mazara del Vallo)
Births 1810-1911: PRO Kew, FO653/12-13.

Messina
Births 1854-1957, deaths 1854-1954: PRO Kew, FO653/14-17.
Bap 1902-8: Guildhall Library, Ms 23627.
Bur 1877-9: Guildhall Library, Ms 23609.

For addresses of repositories see page 2

For other sources which may relate to places on this page see 'How to use this guide' (page 1)

Milazzo
Deaths 1887-1903: PRO Kew, FO653/18.

Naples
Bap, mar and bur 1817-22: PRO Chancery Lane, RG33/118 (index to bap in RG43/1, mar in RG43/7, bur in RG43/3).
Bap 1830-60, mar and bur 1831-60: Guildhall Library, Ms 11209 (index, except 1855, in Ms 15061/1-2).
Bap, mar and bur 1835-6: PRO Chancery Lane, in RG33/155 (index to bap in RG43/1, mar in RG43/7, bur in RG43/3).

Palermo
Bap 1819-66, mar 1817-77, bur 1820-75: Guildhall Library, Ms 24117.
Births 1837-91, 1932-40, deaths 1850-1919: PRO Kew, FO653/19-21.

Pegli
Bap 1875-1909, mar 1880, bur 1875-1971: United Society for the Propagation of the Gospel.

Pisa
Bap 1848: Guildhall Library, in Ms 20996.
Mar 1881-2: Guildhall Library, in Ms 22918.
Mar 1887-1901: Guildhall Library, in Ms 22914.
Bur 1872-1932: Guildhall Library, in Ms 23783.

Porto Empedocle
Births 1906: PRO Kew, FO653/22.

Rome
Bap and mar 1816-52 (Rome and Tuscany): PRO Kew, FO170/6.
Bap and bur 1825-6: Lambeth Palace Library, in Fulham papers Howley vol 4.
Bap 1826-69, mar 1835-65, bur 1825-69: Guildhall Library, Ms 11208 (index in Ms 15061/1-2).
Bap 1867-1944, mar 1870-1939, bur 1868-1941: Society of Genealogists.
Bap, mar and bur 1875-7: Guildhall Library, Ms 20991.
Mar 1872-89: PRO Chancery Lane, RG33/119 (index in RG43/7).
Bur 1901: Guildhall Library, in Ms 21473.

San Remo
Bap 1867-76, bur 1865-75: Guildhall Library, Ms 20992.

For addresses of repositories see page 2

For other sources which may relate to places on this page see 'How to use this guide' (page 1)

Savona
Bur 1921-37: Guildhall Library, in Ms 23626.

Sicily
Births 1810-1957, deaths 1847-1957: PRO Kew, FO653/2-28 and FO720/1.
Bap 1838: PRO Chancery Lane, in RG33/155 (index in RG43/1).

Syracuse
Births 1909-18, deaths 1912-19, 1953-7: PRO Kew, FO653/23-5.

Taormina
Bap 1920, bur 1914: Guildhall Library, in Ms 23629.
Deaths 1909-22: PRO Kew, FO653/26.

Terranova: see *Gela*

Trapani
Births 1871-1927: PRO Kew, FO653/27-8.

Trieste
Bap 1828: Guildhall Library, in Ms 11226.
Bap 1861-5, mar 1862-4, bur 1862-5: Guildhall Library, Ms 20993.
Mar 1835: Guildhall Library, in Ms 11219 (index in Ms 15061/1-2).

Turin
Bap 1830 and 1836: Guildhall Library, in Ms 11219 (index in Ms 15061/1-2).
Bap and bur 1866-7: Guildhall Library, Ms 11830 (index in Ms 15061/1-2).
Mar 1858-64: PRO Chancery Lane, RG33/120 (index in RG43/7).

Tuscany: see *Rome;* see also *Florence, Leghorn* and *Pisa*

Venice
Bap 1856-79, mar 1874-9, bur 1871-9: Guildhall Library, Ms 20997.
Mar 1874-1947: PRO Chancery Lane, RG33/121 (index in RG43/7).

Viareggio
Bap, mar and bur 1902-10: Guildhall Library, in Ms 23784/1.
Bap, mar and bur 1912-27: Guildhall Library, in Ms 23784/2.
Bap, mar and bur 1927-60: Guildhall Library, in Ms 23784/3.
A few mar 1920-5 also entered in Guildhall Library Mss 23776 and 23783.
Bur 1881-2, 1912-c.1936: Guildhall Library, in Ms 23783.

For addresses of repositories see page 2

For other sources which may relate to places on this
page see 'How to use this guide' (page 1)

JAMAICA: see WEST INDIES

JAPAN
General
Mar 1860-99 listed in Neil Pedlar, *An Indexed List of British Marriages Solemnised during Extraterritoriality 1860-1899 in Japan* (Newquay, 1993) (not available at Guildhall Library).
Mar 1860-99 (as above): Society of Genealogists.
Some entries for mar 1867-90 in 'International memoranda' at Guildhall Library: see page 6.

Kobe
Bap 1874-1941, mar 1874-1939, bur 1902-41: PRO Chancery Lane, RG33/122-6 (index in RG43/1-3, 6-8, 10-14).

Nagasaki
Births 1864-1940, mar 1922-40, deaths 1859-1940: PRO Kew, FO796/236-8.

Osaka
Mar 1892-1904: PRO Chancery Lane, RG33/127-30.

Shimonoseki
Births 1903-21, mar 1906-22, deaths 1903-21: PRO Kew, FO797/48-50.

Tokyo
Mar 1870-87: PRO Kew, in FO345/34.

Yokohama
Mar 1870-87: PRO Kew, in FO345/34.
Bur 1854-1980 listed in Neil Pedlar, *An Indexed List of British Marriages Solemnised during Extraterritoriality 1860-1899 in Japan* (Newquay, 1993) (not available at Guildhall Library).
Bur 1854-1980 (as above): Society of Genealogists.

JAVA: see INDONESIA

KENYA
Births 1905-24: PRO Chancery Lane, in RG36 (index in RG43/18).

For addresses of repositories see page 2

For other sources which may relate to places on this page see 'How to use this guide' (page 1)

KOREA
Births and bap 1960: Guildhall Library, Ms 29444.

KUWAIT
Bur 1909-35: Society of Genealogists.
Births, mar and deaths 1937-61: India Office Library, N/12/1-16.

LATVIA: see RUSSIA

LEBANON
Beirut
Mar 1859-1939: PRO Kew, FO616/5.

LIBYA
Tripoli
Bap 1819 in 'International memoranda' at Guildhall Library: see page 6.
Mar 1931-40, deaths 1938-9: PRO Kew, FO161/7.

LITHUANIA: see RUSSIA

LUXEMBOURG
Bap, mar, bur 1958-date: Luxembourg Anglican Chaplaincy, details available from Guildhall Library.

MACAO: see CHINA

MADAGASCAR (MALAGASY REPUBLIC)
Antananarive: see *Tananarive*

Antseranan: see *Diego Suarez*

Diego Suarez (Antseranan)
Births 1907-21: PRO Kew, FO711/1.

Tamatave
Mar 1890 in 'International memoranda' at Guildhall Library: see page 6.
Mar 1891: Guildhall Library, in Ms 20996.
Deaths 1935-40: PRO Kew, FO714/1.

For addresses of repositories see page 2

For other sources which may relate to places on this
page see 'How to use this guide' (page 1)

Tananarive (Antananarive)
Births 1865-8: PRO Kew, FO710/1.
Mar 1876-83 in 'International memoranda' at Guildhall Library: see page 6.

MADEIRA: see **PORTUGAL**

MALAGASY REPUBLIC: see **MADAGASCAR**

MALAWI: see **NYASALAND**

MALAYA

Bap, mar and bur in the East India Company's establishment at Penang (Prince of Wales Island), Malacca and Singapore 1799-1829: India Office Library, N/8/1 (index in Z/N/8/1). Later bap, mar and bur to c.1867 included in main series of Indian registers at India Office Library: see **INDIA**.
Births, mar and deaths in the East India Company's establishment at Penang (Prince of Wales Island), Malacca and Singapore 1807-32: printed in *East India Register* 1809-33 (generally under 'Prince of Wales Island').
Some entries for mar 1883-6 in 'International memoranda' at Guildhall Library: see page 6.
Births, mar and deaths 1915-c.1946: PRO Chancery Lane, in RG36 (index in RG43/18).
Births 1920-48: PRO Chancery Lane, RG33/131 (index in RG43/1).
Deaths 1941-5: PRO Chancery Lane, in RG33/132 (index in RG43/14).

Singapore
Bap 1823-70, mar 1826-70, bur 1820-75: Society of Genealogists.

MALAYSIA: see MALAYA, NORTH BORNEO and SARAWAK

MALTA

Most registers are held locally in Malta. Guildhall Library has details of registers (bap, mar, bur 1801-date) held in the Anglican Chaplaincies of Sliema and Valletta (St Paul's Anglican Pro-Cathedral). The following are available in the United Kingdom:

Bap 1801-7, mar 1801-70, bur 1801-3: Society of Genealogists.
Military bap, mar and bur extracts 1801-18: Society of Genealogists.
Some entries for bap 1806-14, mar 1817 in 'International memoranda' at Guildhall Library: see page 6.

For addresses of repositories see page 2

For other sources which may relate to places on this page see 'How to use this guide' (page 1)

Military bap (Mediterranean fleet) 1933-8: Greater London Record Office.
Mar 1801-92: Lambeth Palace Library, Mss 1470-1.
Mar 1904-36: PRO Kew, FO161/7.
Bur 1857-99: Society of Genealogists.

MESOPOTAMIA: see IRAQ

MEXICO
Mexico City
Births and deaths 1854-67: PRO Kew, FO723/1-2.
Bur 1827-1926: PRO Kew, FO207/58.
Bur 1861-1949: Society of Genealogists.

Vera Cruz
Births, deaths and bur 1858-67: PRO Chancery Lane, RG33/140 (index to births in RG43/1, deaths and bur in RG43/3).

MINORCA: see SPAIN, *Balearic Islands*

MONACO: see FRANCE

MONTSERRAT: see WEST INDIES

MOROCCO
General
Some bap post 1920 in the Bishop of Gilbraltar's memorandum book at Guildhall Library: see page 6.

Daralbaida
Bap 1898 in 'International memoranda' at Guildhall Library: see page 6.

Tangier
Bap 1874: Guildhall Library, in Ms 20996.

NETHERLANDS (HOLLAND)
General
Scottish military bap and mar 1708-83: printed in *Scottish History Society* 1st series vol 38 (1901).
Many entries in 'Miscellaneous' series 1826-1951 at PRO Chancery Lane,

---

For addresses of repositories see page 2

For other sources which may relate to places on this page see 'How to use this guide' (page 1)

(see page 9); the series also includes a separate death register for the Netherlands and its colonies 1839-71 (RG35/17).
Scottish military mar 1574-1665; printed in J. Maclean, *De Huwelkijksintekeningen van Schotse Militarien in Nederland* (Zutphen, 1976) (not available at Guildhall Library).
Some entries for mar 1819-89 in 'International memoranda' at Guildhall Library: see page 6.
The registers of most English churches in the Netherlands are held in the Municipal Archives of the town or city where the church was situated; some are noted below. The following list includes those available in the United Kingdom:

Cadzand
Walloon bap 1685-1724, mar extracts 1616-61, mar 1686-1723: Society of Genealogists.

Crooswijk
Bur 1882-1931: Gemeentelijke Archiefdienst (Municipal Archives), Robert Fruinstreet 52, POB 25082, 3001 HB Rotterdam, Netherlands.

Delft
Bap 1643-1723, mar 1646-96: New College Library, Edinburgh, Ms DEL.
Bap 1644 and 1655, mar 1647, 1650 and 1659: printed in W. Stevens, *History of the Scottish Church, Rotterdam* (Edinburgh, 1832) page 296 (not available at Guildhall Library).

Hague, The
Bap 1627-1821, births 1837-9 and 1859-94, mar 1627-1889, deaths 1859-1907: PRO Chancery Lane, RG33/83-8 (index to bap and births in RG43/1, mar in RG43/7, deaths in RG43/3).
Bap 1815-25: printed in *The Genealogist* New series vol 26 (1910).
Bap 1851 in 'International memoranda' at Guildhall Library. see page 6.

Leiden
Mar 1576-1640 in Johanna H. Tammel, *The Pilgrims and other people from the British Isles in Leiden, 1576-1640* (Peel, Isle of Man, 1989).

Rotterdam
Index to mar 1576-1811: in *Family History* vol 13 (1985-6).
Bap and mar 1708-94: PRO Chancery Lane, RG33/89 (index to bap in RG43/1, mar in RG43/7).

For addresses of repositories see page 2

For other sources which may relate to places on this page see 'How to use this guide' (page 1)

Bap 1708-1887, mar 1708-1951, bur 1708-1907: Gemeentelijke Archiefdienst (Municipal Archives), Robert Fruinstreet 52, POB 25082, 3001 HB Rotterdam, Netherlands.
Bap 1815-16, mar 1816, bur 1815-16: Guildhall Library, Ms 11200 (index in Ms 15061/1-2).
Mar 1576-1811: Society of Genealogists.

Schiedam
Bur 1882-1931: Gemeentelijke Archiefdienst, Robert Fruinstreet 52, POB 25082, 3001 HB Rotterdam, Netherlands.

Vlaardingen
Bur 1882-1931: Gemeentelijke Archiefdienst, Robert Fruinstreet 52, POB 25082, 3001 HB Rotterdam, Netherlands.

NEVIS: see WEST INDIES

NEWFOUNDLAND: see CANADA

NEW GUINEA
Deaths 1888-1906: Society of Genealogists.

NEW ZEALAND
All original church registers are held locally in New Zealand.

Enquiries about civil registration records (from 1848) should be addressed to the Registrar General of Births, Deaths and Marriages, PO Box 31-115, Lower Hutt, New Zealand.

For records of emigration to New Zealand see page 12.

For New Zealand sources other than church registers see Anne Bromell, *Tracing Family History in New Zealand* (Wellington, 1988) and *Family History at National Archives* (Wellington, 1990) (latter not available at Guildhall Library). Limited assistance is available, in return for a donation, from the New Zealand Society of Genealogists, PO Box 8795, Symonds Street, Auckland 1035, New Zealand.

Births and mar 1840-1920, deaths 1848-1920: Society of Genealogists.
Index to Congregational mar 1864-1920: Society of Genealogists.

For addresses of repositories see page 2

For other sources which may relate to places on this page see 'How to use this guide' (page 1)

Index to Associated Churches of Christ mar 1873-1920: Society of Genealogists.

Dunedin
Index to mar 1852-1920: Society of Genealogists.

Fielding
Births, mar and deaths extracts 1882-1909: Society of Genealogists.

Hawera
Births 1880-1982: Society of Genealogists.

Lyttelton
Births extracts 1851-65, mar 1851-80, deaths extracts 1851-65: Society of Genealogists.

Nelson
Births, mar and deaths 1880-5: Society of Genealogists.

Ruapuke Island
Index to mar 1844-82: Society of Genealogists.

Waikouaiti
Index to Wesleyan mar 1841-57: Society of Genealogists.

Wanganui
Births, mar and deaths 1845-1940: Society of Genealogists.

Wellington
Deaths 1840-7: Society of Genealogists.

NORTH BORNEO (SABAH)
Births, mar and deaths 1923-c.1946: PRO Chancery Lane, in RG36 (index in RG43/18).
Deaths 1941-5: PRO Chancery Lane, in RG33/132 (index in RG43/14).

NORWAY
Bodo
Births 1888-90, deaths 1895: PRO Kew, FO724/1-2.

For addresses of repositories see page 2

For other sources which may relate to places on this page see 'How to use this guide' (page 1)

Christiania: see *Oslo*

Drammen
Deaths 1906: PRO Kew, FO532/2.

Kragero
Deaths 1895: PRO Kew, FO725/1.

Lofoten Islands
Births 1850-1932: PRO Kew, FO529/8-10 and FO726/1.

Oslo (Christiania)
Births 1850-1936, mar 1853-1936, deaths 1850-1936: PRO Kew, FO236/60-6 and FO529/3, 11-14.

Porsgrunn
Births 1885-91: PRO Kew, FO531/2.

NYASALAND (MALAWI)
Births 1904-c.1950: PRO Chancery Lane, in RG36 (partial index in RG43/18).

PAKISTAN: see INDIA

PALESTINE (ISRAEL)
General
Births and deaths 1920-35: PRO Chancery Lane, RG33/141 (index in RG43/17).
Births and deaths 1936-48: PRO Chancery Lane, in RG36 (partial index in RG43/18).

Haifa
Church of Scotland bap 1945-8, mar 1943-7: National Library of Scotland, Acc 7548/G71-2.

Jaffa (Tel Aviv)
Births 1900-14: PRO Kew, FO734/1.
Church of Scotland mar 1936-51: National Library of Scotland, Acc 7548/G77-8.

For addresses of repositories see page 2

For other sources which may relate to places on this page see 'How to use this guide' (page 1)

Jerusalem
Births 1850-1921, deaths 1851-1914: PRO Kew, FO617/3-5.
Military bap 1939-47: PRO Kew, WO156/6.

Sarafand
Military bap 1940-6, banns 1944-7: PRO Kew, WO156/7-8.

PAPUA NEW GUINEA: see NEW GUINEA

PERSIA: see IRAN

PERU
Some entries for bap 1825-44, mar 1835-71 in 'International memoranda' at Guildhall Library: see page 6.
Births 1837-41, mar 1827 and 1836, deaths 1837-41: PRO Chancery Lane, in RG33/155 (index to births in RG43/1, mar in RG43/7, deaths in RG43/3).

PHILIPPINES
Bap 1872 in 'International memoranda' at Guildhall Library: see page 6.

PITCAIRN ISLAND
Births, mar and deaths 1790-1854: Society for Promoting Christian Knowledge. Printed by the Society as *The Pitcairn Island Register Book* (London, 1929) (not available at Guildhall Library).

POLAND
Breslau (Wroclaw)
Births 1929-38, deaths 1932-8: PRO Kew, FO715/1-2.

Danzig (Gdansk)
Bap and mar 1706-1811: Lambeth Palace Library, Ms 1847.
Births 1851-1910, deaths 1850-1914: PRO Kew, FO634/16-18.

Gdansk: see *Danzig*

Lodz
Births 1925-39: PRO Kew, FO869/1.

Silesia
Bap 1888 in 'International memoranda' at Guildhall Library: see page 6.

For addresses of repositories see page 2

For other sources which may relate to places on this page see 'How to use this guide' (page 1)

Stettin (Szczecin)
Births 1864-1939, deaths 1857-1933: PRO Kew, FO719/1-2.
Mar 1855 in 'International memoranda' at Guildhall Library: see page 6.

Warsaw
Bap, mar and bur 1858-61: Guildhall Library, Ms 11197A (index in Ms 15061/1-2).
Bap 1951-3: Guildhall Library, in Ms 11225.

Wroclaw: see *Breslau*

PORTUGAL

General
Some entries for bap 1811-48, mar 1812-90 in 'International memoranda' at Guildhall Library: see page 6.
Some bap post 1920 in the Bishop of Gibraltar's memorandam book at Guildhall Library: see page 6.

Azores, Ponta Delgada
Births, bap, mar, deaths and bur 1807-66: PRO Kew, FO599/1.
Bap and mar 1827-49, bur 1827-48: Guildhall Library, in Ms 10446E (index in Ms 15061/1-2, under 'Ponta Delgada').
Bap 1827-1902: Guildhall Library, Ms 23643.
Bap, mar and bur 1835-7: PRO Chancery Lane, in RG33/155 (index to bap in RG43/1, mar in RG43/7, bur in RG43/3).
Mar 1827-62 and 1945: Guildhall Library, Ms 23644.
Bur 1827-1955: Guildhall Library, Ms 23645.

Funchal: see *Madeira*

Lisbon
Bap 1721-93, mar 1721-94, bur 1721-93: Guildhall Library, Ms 10446/1 (index in Ms 10446/5).
Congregational bap, mar and bur 1781-1807: Society of Genealogists.
Bap, mar and bur 1794-1807: Guildhall Library, Ms 10446/4 (index to bap and mar to 1807 and bur to 1799 in Ms 10446/5).
Bap and mar 1812-date, bur 1811-date: Lisbon Anglican Chaplaincy, details available from Guildhall Library.
Mar 1721-1863: Society of Genealogists.
Index to mar 1721-1940: Society of Genealogists.
Mar 'at a distance from Lisbon' 1764, 1780-1 and 1797-9: Guildhall Library, Ms 10446/3 (index in Ms 10446/5).

For addresses of repositories see page 2

For other sources which may relate to places on this
page see 'How to use this guide' (page 1)

Mar 1765-83: Guildhall Library, Ms 10446/2 (index in Ms 10446/5).
Mar 1822-59: Office of Population Censuses and Surveys (index at PRO Chancery Lane, in RG43/7).
Mar 1859-76: PRO Kew, FO173/8.

Madeira
Births, bap, mar and deaths 1848-date: Madeira Anglican Chaplaincy, details available from Guildhall Library.
Bap and bur 1848-51: Guildhall Library, Ms 10446F (index in Ms 15061/1-2, under 'Funchal').

Oporto
Bap 1717-89, mar 1716-97, bur 1716-25 and 1784-7: Guildhall Library, Ms 10446A (index in Ms 15061/1-2, under 'Portugal'); printed in C. Sellers, *Oporto Old and New* (London, 1899).
Bap 1778-1807, mar 1799-1804, bur 1788-1807: Guildhall Library, Ms 10446B/1 (index in Ms 15061/1-2, under 'Portugal').
Bap, mar and bur 1814-74: PRO Chancery Lane, RG33/142 (index to bap in RG43/1, mar in RG43/7, bur in RG43/3).
Bap 1814-32, mar 1814-31, bur 1814-32: Guildhall Library, Ms 10446B/2 (index in Ms 15061/1-2, under 'Portugal').
Bap 1832-65, mar 1833-64, bur 1832-65: Guildhall Library, Ms 10,446B/3 (index in Ms 15061/1-2, under 'Portugal').
Bap, mar and bur 1833: PRO Chancery Lane, in RG33/155 (index to bap in RG43/1, mar in RG43/7, bur in RG43/3).
Bap, mar and bur 1878-98: Guildhall Library, Ms 20994.
Bap 1905-7, mar 1905-6, bur 1905-7: Guildhall Library, Ms 10446C (index in Ms 15061/1-2, under 'Portugal').
Bap 1907-89: Guildhall Library, Ms 24131.
Mar 1908-89: Guildhall Library, Ms 24132.
Bur 1876-1912: printed in *Miscellanea Genealogica et Heraldica* 5th series vol 1 (1916).
Bur 1907-90: Guildhall Library, Ms 24133.

Ponta Delgada: see *Azores*

St Vincent
Mar 1894-1922: PRO Kew, FO767/6.

REUNION
Mar 1864-1921: PRO Kew, FO322/1-2.

For addresses of repositories see page 2

For other sources which may relate to places on this page see 'How to use this guide' (page 1)

ROUMANIA

General
Some bap post 1920 in the Bishop of Gibraltar's memorandum book at Guildhall Library: see page 6.

Braila
Bap 1899-1903, mar and bur 1899-1905: Guildhall Library, in Ms 23634/1.
Bap 1903-5: Guildhall Library, in Ms 23634/2.
Births 1922-30, deaths 1921-9: PRO Kew, FO727/1-2.

Bucharest
Births 1851-1931, bap 1858-1948, deaths 1854-1929: PRO Kew, FO625/2-4, 6.
Bap and bur 1879: Guildhall Library, in Ms 20996.
Bap 1899-1903, mar and bur 1899-1905: Guildhall Library, in Ms 23634/1.
Bap 1903-5: Guildhall Library, in Ms 23634/2.
Bap, mar, bur 1905-80: Guildhall Library, in Ms 24120/1-3.
Mar 1880-3 in 'International memoranda' at Guildhall Library: see page 6.
Banns 1914-68: Guildhall Library, Ms 24118.
Bur 1862-1986: Guildhall Library, Ms 24119.

Constanta (Kustendje)
Bap 1864: Guildhall Library, in Ms 20996.
Births and deaths 1862-73: PRO Kew, FO887/1-2.
Bap 1899-1903, mar and bur 1899-1905: Guildhall Library, in Ms 23634/1.
Bap 1903-5: Guildhall Library, in Ms 23634/2.

Galatz
Bap 1864: Guildhall Library, in Ms 20996.
Bap 1899-1903, mar and bur 1899-1905: Guildhall Library, in Ms 23634/1.
Bap 1903-5: Guildhall Library, in Ms 23634/2.
Mar 1891-1939: PRO Kew, FO517/1-2.

Kustendje: see *Constanta*

Lower Danube
Bap 1869-1907: PRO Kew, FO625/4.
Mar 1868-1914: PRO Chancery Lane, RG33/143 (index in RG43/7).
Bur 1869-70: PRO Kew, FO786/120.

For addresses of repositories see page 2

For other sources which may relate to places on this page see 'How to use this guide' (page 1)

Sulina

Births 1861-1932, deaths 1860-1931: PRO Kew, FO728/1-2 and FO886/ 1-2.
Bap 1885, 1899-1903, mar and bur 1899-1905: Guildhall Library, in Ms 23634/1.
Bap 1903-5: Guildhall Library, in Ms 23634/2.

RUSSIA (SOVIET UNION)

General

Many entries in 'Miscellaneous' series 1826-1951 at PRO Chancery Lane (see page 9); the series also includes separate registers of births, mar and deaths for Russia 1835-70 (RG35/18-19).
Some bap post 1920 in the Bishop of Gibraltar's memorandum book at Guildhall Library: see page 6.
Some entries for bap 1926-37 in Helsinki registers at Guildhall Library: see under **FINLAND**.

Archangel

Bap and bur 1719: Guildhall Library, Ms 11192B (with index at back); also indexed in Ms 15061/1-2, under 'Petersburg'.
Bap 1833-83, mar 1834-74, bur 1833-5 and 1879: Guildhall Library, Ms 11195 (index in Ms 15061/1-2).
Births 1849-1909, mar 1849-61, deaths 1849-1915: PRO Kew, FO267/44-6.
Bap 1915-18, mar 1915-19, bur 1913-19: Guildhall Library, in Ms 11195C.
Transcript: Ms 11195B (index in Ms 15061/1-2).
Mar 1819: Guildhall Library, Ms 11195C.
Bur 1835-76: Guildhall Library, Ms 11195A (index in Ms 15061/1-2). Bur 1866 also in Ms 11195C.

Batum

Births 1884-1921, mar 1891-1920, deaths 1884-1920: PRO Kew, FO397/1-2, 5-6.

Cronstadt (Kronstadt)

Bap, mar and bur 1807-49: Guildhall Library, Ms 11196/1 (index in Ms 15061/1-2).
Bap 1850-94, mar 1850-87, bur 1850-94: Guildhall Library, Ms 11196/2 (index in Ms 15061/1-2).

Donetsk: see *Hughesovka*

For addresses of repositories see page 2

For other sources which may relate to places on this
page see 'How to use this guide' (page 1)

Ekaterinburg (Sverdlovsk)
Deaths 1918-19: PRO Kew, FO399/5.

Estonia
Some entries for bap 1922-37, mar 1924-30, banns 1926-30, bur 1926-33 in Helsinki registers at Guildhall Library: see under **FINLAND.**

Estonia, Pernau
Births 1894-1930, deaths 1894-1933: PRO Kew, FO399/11-12.

Estonia, Tallinn (Reval)
Births 1866-1940, mar 1921-39, deaths 1875-1940: PRO Kew, FO514/1-2, 7-9.

Feodosiya: see *Theodosia*

Hughesovka (Donetsk)
Bap 1902-17, mar 1904-14, bur 1902-16: Guildhall Library, in Ms 23646.

Kaliningrad: see *Konigsberg*

Kaunas: see *Lithuania*

Klaipeda: see *Lithuania*

Konigsberg (Kaliningrad)
Births 1869-1933, mar 1864-1904, deaths 1857-1932: PRO Kew, FO509/1-4.

Kovno: see *Lithuania*

Kronstadt: see *Cronstadt*

Latvia, Libau (Leipaja)
Births 1883-1932, deaths 1871-1932: PRO Kew, FO440/10 and FO661/4- 5.
Bap 1893-1928: Guildhall Library, Ms 10953C/1.
Mar 1892-1905: Guildhall Library, Ms 10953C/2. Duplicate: Ms 10953C/3.
Banns 1896-1911: Guildhall Library, Ms 10953C/4.
Bur 1898-1915: Guildhall Library, Ms 10953C/5.

Latvia, Riga
Bap 1830-1938: Guildhall Library, Ms 10953. Bap 1921-2 also in Ms 10953B/1 (index to bap 1921-2 in Ms 15061/1-2).

For addresses of repositories see page 2

For other sources which may relate to places on this page see 'How to use this guide' (page 1)

Births 1850-1910, deaths 1850-1915: PRO Kew, FO377/3-4.
Births 1921-40, mar 1920-8, deaths 1921-40: PRO Kew, FO516/1-2, 8-9.
Mar 1831-1937: Guildhall Library, Ms 10953A. Mar 1921 also in Ms 10953B/1 (index to mar 1921 in Ms 15061/1-2).
Bur 1830-1939: Guildhall Library, Ms 10953B/2.

Latvia, Windau
Births 1906-9: PRO Kew, FO399/19.

Leipaja: see *Latvia, Libau*

Leningrad: see *St Petersburg*

Libau: see *Latvia*

Lithuania, Kovno (Kaunas)
Births 1927-40, deaths 1922-40: PRO Kew, FO722/2-3.

Lithuania, Memel (Klaipeda)
Births 1924-5, deaths 1923-8: PRO Kew, FO722/1, 4.

Memel: see *Lithuania*

Moscow
Bap, mar and bur 1706-23: Guildhall Library, in Ms 11192B (with index at back; also indexed in Ms 15061/1-2, under 'Petersburg').
Bap, mar and bur 1825-1920: Guildhall Library, as follows:
Registers: bap, mar and bur 1825-61: Ms 11192C
              bap, mar and bur 1861-80: Ms 11192A
              bap 1880-1920: Ms 11192/1
              mar 1880-1920: Ms 11192/2
              bur 1880-1920: Ms 11192/3
Transcripts (all indexed in Ms 15061/1-2):
              bap 1825-64, mar 1826-64, bur 1825-64: Ms 11193/1
              bap, mar and bur 1865-83: Ms 11193/2 part I
              bap, mar and bur 1884-96: Ms 11193/2 part II
              bap, mar and bur 1897-1907: Ms 11193/3 part I
              bap, mar and bur 1908-19: Ms 11193/3 part II.
Births 1882-1919, mar 1894-1924, deaths 1881-1918: PRO Kew, FO518/1-4.

For addresses of repositories see page 2

For other sources which may relate to places on this page see 'How to use this guide' (page 1)

Mar 1826-58: Office of Population Censuses and Surveys (index at PRO Chancery Lane, in RG43/7).

Nicolayev
Births 1872-1917, deaths 1874-1915: PRO Kew, FO399/7-8.

Novorossiysk
Births 1911-20, deaths 1896-1920: PRO Kew, FO399/9-10.

Odessa
Bap 1818, mar 1821 in 'International memoranda' at Guildhall Library: see page 6.
Births 1852-1919, mar 1851-1916, deaths 1852-1919: PRO Kew, FO359/3-12.
Bap 1865-86: Scottish Record Office, CH3/249/1.
Bap 1883-1908, mar 1884-91: Guildhall Library, Ms 11197/1.
Bap 1892-1918, mar 1892-1917: Guildhall Library, Ms 11197/2.
Mar 1869-80: Scottish Record Office, CH3/249/2.
Banns 1905-17: Guildhall Library, Ms 11197/3.
Bur 1883-1901: Guildhall Library, Ms 11197/4.
Bur 1906-18: Guildhall Library, Ms 11197/5.

Pernau: see *Estonia*

Petrograd: see *St Petersburg*

Poti
Births 1871-1906, deaths 1871-1920: PRO Kew, FO399/13-14.

Reval: see *Estonia*

Riga: see *Latvia*

Rostov-on-Don
Births 1891-1914, mar 1904-18, deaths 1906-16: PRO Kew, FO398/1-2, 8-9.

St Petersburg (Petrograd, Leningrad)
Bap, mar and bur 1723-7 and 1737-1815: Guildhall Library, in Ms 11192B (index at back; also indexed in Ms 15061/1-2, under 'Petersburg').

For addresses of repositories see page 2

For other sources which may relate to places on this page see 'How to use this guide' (page 1)

Bap, mar and bur 1816-1918: Guildhall Library, as follows (all indexed in Ms 15061/1-2, under 'Petersburg'):

1816-28: Ms 11194/1 part I	1882-6: Ms 11194/3 part III
1830-9: Ms 11194/1 part II	1887-93 and 1895: Ms 11194/3 part IV
1840-9: Ms 11194/1 part III	1894 and 1896-1901:Ms 11194/4 part I
1850-6: Ms 11194/2 part I	1902-12: Ms 11194/4 part II
1857-62: Ms 11194/2 part II	1912-18: Ms 11194/4 part III.
1863-7: Ms 11194/2 part III	
1868-77: Ms 11194/3 part I	
1878-81: Ms 11194/3 part II	

Independent church bap 1818-40, bur 1821-40: PRO Chancery Lane, RG4/4605 (index to bap in RG43/1, bur in RG43/3).

Bap 1826 in 'International memoranda' at Guildhall Library: see page 6.

Births, bap, mar, and bur 1840-1918, deaths 1840-1914: PRO Chancery Lane, RG33/144-52 (index 1886-1917 in RG33/162; also index to births and bap in RG43/1, mar in RG43/7, deaths and bur in RG43/3).

Births 1856-1938, mar 1892-1917, deaths 1897-1927: PRO Kew, FO378/3-9.

Sebastopol
Births 1886-98, mar 1910, deaths 1893-1908: PRO Kew, FO399/3, 15-16.

Sverdlovsk: see *Ekaterinburg*

Tallinn: see *Estonia*

Theodosia (Feodosiya)
Births 1904-6, deaths 1907-18: PRO Kew, FO 399/17-18.

Vladivostok
Births 1911-27, mar 1916-23, deaths 1908-24: PRO Kew, FO510/1-2, 4, 10.

Vyborg
Births 1924-31, deaths 1929-37: PRO Kew, FO757/1-3.

Windau: see *Latvia*

SABAH: see NORTH BORNEO

ST CHRISTOPHER: see WEST INDIES

ST HELENA

Bap, mar and bur 1767-1835: India Office Library, N/6/1-3 (index in Z/N/6/1).

For addresses of repositories see page 2

For other sources which may relate to places on this page see 'How to use this guide' (page 1)

ST KITTS: see WEST INDIES, *St Christopher*

ST LUCIA: see WEST INDIES

ST VINCENT: see WEST INDIES

SAMOA
Bap 1877 in 'International memoranda' at Guildhall Library: see page 6.

SARAWAK
Bap 1848-1951, births 1910-49, mar 1844-1953: Society of Genealogists.
Bap, mar and bur 1848-52: Guildhall Library, Ms 11220 (index in Ms 15061/1-2).
Births, mar and deaths 1910-c.1946: PRO Chancery Lane, in RG36 (index in RG43/18).
Deaths 1941-5: PRO Chancery Lane, in RG33/132 (index in RG43/14).

SICILY: see ITALY

SINGAPORE: see MALAYA

SOMALILAND (SOMALIA)
Births 1905-20: PRO Chancery Lane, in RG36 (index in RG43/18).

SOUTH AFRICA
General
A very few registers or register transcripts are available in the United Kingdom (see below), but almost all original church registers are held locally in South Africa.

For biographical details of early British settlers (before c.1826) see E. Morse Jones, *Roll of the British settlers in South Africa* (Capetown, 1971). See also P. Philip, *British residents at the Cape* 1795-1819 (Capetown, 1981).

Enquiries about civil registration records (from 1838, but incomplete until early 20th century) should be addressed to the Registrar of Births, Marriages and Deaths, Department of Home Affairs, Private Bag XII4, Pretoria, 0001, South Africa. Some further records of births 1696-1919, mar 1696-1913 and deaths 1689-1932 are available on microfilm at the Transvaal Archives Depot, Private Bag X236, Pretoria, 0001, South Africa.

For addresses of repositories see page 2

For other sources which may relate to places on this page see 'How to use this guide' (page 1)

British military deaths in the Boer War 1899-1902 are registered at the Office of Population Censuses and Surveys.

For records of emigration to South Africa see page 12.

For further information about South African sources see R. J. T. Lombard, *Handbook for Genealogical Research in South Africa* (Pretoria, 1990) (not available at Guildhall Library).

Cape of Good Hope
Military bap 1795-1803, mar 1796-1803, bur 1795-1803: Guildhall Library, Ms 11569 (index in Ms 15061/1-2).
Bap 1810-21, mar 1806-21: extracts printed in *The Genealogist* New series vol 30 (1914).
Bap 1810-21, mar 1806-21, deaths 1795-1815 (extracts): Society of Genealogists.
Dutch Reformed Church mar extracts, 1813-26: Society of Genealogists.
Deaths 1796-1826: extracts printed in *The Genealogist* New series vol 29 (1913) and vol 32 (1916).

Grahamstown
Baptist bap and mar 1853-60: Society of Genealogists.

Port Elizabeth
Bap, mar and bur 1858-98: Society of Genealogists.

Simonstown
Mar 1862 in 'International memoranda' at Guildhall Library: see page 6.

Zululand, Melmoth
Bap 1896-1982: Society of Genealogists.

SOUTH GEORGIA: see FALKLAND ISLANDS

SOUTH YEMEN: see ADEN

SOVIET UNION: see RUSSIA

SPAIN
General
Some entries for bap 1813-95, mar 1835-88 in 'International memoranda' at Guildhall Library: see page 6.

For addresses of repositories see page 2

For other sources which may relate to places on this page see 'How to use this guide' (page 1)

Some bap post 1920 in the Bishop of Gibraltar's memorandum book at Guildhall Library: see page 6.

Aguilas
Births 1875-1911, deaths 1874-1911: PRO Kew, FO920/1-2.

Alicante
Bap and mar 1729-30: Lambeth Palace Library, in Fulham Papers Gibson vol 2.

Balearic islands, Minorca
Mar 1801 in 'International memoranda' at Guildhall Library: see page 6.

Bilbao
Deaths 1855-70: PRO Kew, FO729/1.

Canary Islands, Las Palmas
Mar 1834: Guildhall Library, Ms 11219 (index in Ms 15061/1-2, under 'Grand Canary').

Cartagena
Births 1847-87, mar 1858-1904, deaths 1855-71: PRO Kew, FO920/3-6.
Bap 1913: Guildhall Library, in Ms 23607.

Garrucha
Births 1876-90, deaths 1883-1905: PRO Kew, FO920/7-8.

Jerez de la Frontera
Bap 1878-1966: Guildhall Library, Ms 21026.
Bur 1873-1977: Guildhall Library, Ms 21027.

Las Palmas: see *Canary islands*

Malaga
Bap and bur 1851-2: Guildhall Library, Ms 20995.

Minas de Riotinto
Bap 1951-7: Guildhall Library, in Ms 23640.
Mar, undated and 1950: Guildhall Library, Ms 23639.
Death, 1933: Guildhall Library, in Ms 23641.

For addresses of repositories see page 2

For other sources which may relate to places on this page see 'How to use this guide' (page 1)

Minorca: see *Balearic islands*

Portman
Births 1907, deaths 1911: PRO Kew, FO920/9-10.

Seville
Bap 1865-79 and 1934, mar 1865-73 and 1930, bur 1865-79 and 1930: Guildhall Library, Ms 21028/1.
Bap 1880-4, bur 1880-91: Guildhall Library, Ms 21028/2.
Bap 1884-95, bur 1891-6: Guildhall Library, Ms 21028/3.
Bap 1896-1931 and 1936, mar 1910-28, bur 1899-1929 and 1931-6: Guildhall Library, Ms 21028/4.
Bap 1956-76, bur 1952-78: Guildhall Library, in Ms 21029.

SRI LANKA: see CEYLON

SUDAN
General
Births, mar and deaths 1906-c.1950: PRO Chancery Lane, in RG36 (partial index in RG43/18).

Atbara
Bap 1938-53, mar 1937-52: Lambeth Palace Library, Mss 2782A-4.

Khartoum
Bap 1902-59, mar 1936-63, bur 1915-36: Lambeth Palace Library, Mss 2660-3.

SUMATRA: see INDONESIA

SURINAM (DUTCH GUIANA)
Paramaribo
Births 1941-51, deaths 1943: PRO Kew, in FO907/22, 31.

SWEDEN
General
Some entries for bap 1820-57, mar 1845-82 in 'International memoranda' at Guildhall Library: see page 6.

For addresses of repositories see page 2

For other sources which may relate to places on this page see 'How to use this guide' (page 1)

Gothenburg
Bap 1774-1919, mar 1774-1939, bur 1832-90: Landsarkivet (State Archives), Geijersgatam 1, Box 3009, 400 10 Gothenburg, Sweden.
Bap 1881-90: PRO Kew, FO818/15.
Mar 1845-91: PRO Chancery Lane, RG33/153 (index in RG43/7).

Hudiksvall
Deaths 1884: PRO Kew, FO730/1.

Oskarshamn
Deaths 1887: PRO Kew, FO731/1.

Sodra Vi
Births, mar and deaths, 1704-1852: Society of Genealogists.

Stockholm
Bap 1856-1907, mar and bur 1859-1907: Guildhall Library, in Ms 22402.
Bap 1916-60: Guildhall Library, Ms 23642.
Births, mar and deaths 1920-38: PRO Kew, FO748.

SWITZERLAND

General
Some entries for bap 1820-1924, mar 1816-90, bur 1869-91 in 'International memoranda' at Guildhall Library: see page 6.
Certificates of mar 1816-33: PRO Kew, FO194/1.

Berne
Bap 1832: Guildhall Library, in Ms 10926B (index in Ms 15061/1-2, under 'Geneva').

Château d'Oex
Bur 1871 and 1889-1946: Society of Genealogists.

Davos
Bap 1928-69: Guildhall Library, Ms 21661.
Mar 1910-28: Guildhall Library, Ms 21662.
Bur 1890-1913: Guildhall Library, Ms 21663.

Geneva
Bap and mar 1556-8, bur 1556-60: printed in J. S. Burn, *Livre des Anglais à Genève* (London, 1831). The original manuscript is held by Archives d'Etat

---

For addresses of repositories see page 2

For other sources which may relate to places on this page see 'How to use this guide' (page 1)

(State Archives), 1 rue de l'Hotel de Ville, 1211 Geneva 3, Switzerland.
Bap 1817-29, mar 1818-29, bur 1817-29: Guildhall Library, Ms 10926A/1 (index in Ms 15061/1-2).
Bap 1835-42, mar 1837-41, bur 1835-42: Guildhall Library, Ms 10926A/2 (index in Ms 15061/1-2). Bap 1835 also in Ms 10926B.
Births 1850-1934, mar 1850-1933, deaths 1850-1923: PRO Kew, FO778/ 13-22.

Lausanne
Bap, mar and bur 1822-date: Lausanne Anglican Chaplaincy, details available from Guildhall Library; see also Michel Jequier, *L'Eglise Anglaise de Lausanne* (Lausanne, 1978).
Bap 1828 and 1841: Guildhall Library, in Ms 10926B (index in Ms 15061/1-2, under 'Geneva').
Births 1886-1948, mar 1887-1947, deaths 1887-1948: PRO Kew, FO910/ 1-18, 20.

Leysin
Bap 1917-18 and 1921: Guildhall Library, in Ms 16945/2.
Bap 1928, deaths 1927-31: Guildhall Library, in Ms 16945/3.
Bap 1940: Guildhall Library, in Ms 16945/4.
Mar 1914: Guildhall Library, in Ms 16945/1.

Lucerne
Bap 1864-8, bur 1863-8: Guildhall Library, in Ms 10926B (index in Ms 15061/1-2).
Bap 1868-1946, 1954 and 1957-65, bur 1868-1961 (including bur at the English cemetery at Meggen): Guildhall Library, Ms 21330. Bap 1884-1905 and bur 1885-1910 also in Ms 21473.
Bap 1864-1922, bur 1863-1921 (including bur at the English cemetery at Meggen): Guildhall Library, Ms 21331.
Bap 1932 and 1951-74 (certificate stubs only): Guildhall Library, Ms 21475.
Mar 1884-1920: Guildhall Library, Ms 21332.
Mar 1893-1927: Guildhall Library, in Ms 21473.
Mar 1913-73: Guildhall Library, Ms 21474.

Meggen: see *Lucerne*

Montreux
Births 1902-39, mar 1927-33, deaths 1903-41: PRO Kew, FO911/1-3.

For addresses of repositories see page 2

For other sources which may relate to places on this page see 'How to use this guide' (page 1)

Nyon
Bap 1834-9: Guildhall Library, in Ms10926B (index in Ms 15061/1-2, under 'Geneva'). Bap 1835-7 also in Ms 10926A/2.

SYRIA
Aleppo
Births 1717-90, deaths 1655-1918 (extracts): Society of Genealogists.
Bap, mar and bur 1756-1800: PRO Chancery Lane, SP110/70. Transcript at Society of Genealogists. Bap, mar and bur 1756-81 also printed in *The Pedigree Register* vol 3 (1914-15).
Bur 1653-1906: Society of Genealogists.

Damascus
Bap 1845 in 'International memoranda' at Guildhall Library: see page 6.
Births 1934-5, deaths 1935: PRO Kew, FO684/16-17.

TAHITI
Papeete
Births 1818-1948, mar 1845-1941, deaths 1845-1936: PRO Kew, FO687/ 23-34.

TAIWAN: see CHINA

TOBAGO: see WEST INDIES

TRINIDAD: see WEST INDIES

TRISTAN DA CUNHA
Mar 1871-1951, deaths 1892-1949: PRO Kew, PRO30/65/2-3.
Note. A register of births and bap 1867-1955 (i.e. PRO30/65/1) was returned to Tristan da Cunha in 1982.

TUNISIA
Births 1885-8, deaths 1894-1931: PRO Kew, FO870-5 and FO878/1-2.

TURKEY
General
Some entries for bap 1823-8, mar 1821-90 in 'International memoranda' at Guildhall Library: see page 6.

For addresses of repositories see page 2

For other sources which may relate to places on this page see 'How to use this guide' (page 1)

Adana
Mar 1913, 1942 and 1946: PRO Kew, FO609/1-3.

Adrianople (Edirne)
Births 1888-1912, mar 1887-1905: PRO Kew, FO783/3-4.

Ankara (Angora)
Births 1895-1909: PRO Kew, FO732/1.

Bournabat (Bornova)
Bap 1924-date, mar 1926-date, bur 1990-date: Smyrna Anglican Chaplaincy, details available from Guildhall Library.
Bur 1926-90: Guildhall Library, Ms 29744.

Budjah (Buca)
Bap, mar 1866-1958: Smyrna Anglican Chaplaincy, details available from Guildhall Library.

Constantinople (Istanbul)
Bap, mar and bur 1835-6: Guildhall Library, in Ms 10446E (index in Ms 15061/1-2).
Bap 1859-74: Church Missionary Society.
Bap 1860-4, 1868 and 1878, mar 1860-2, bur 1868: Guildhall Library, Ms 20998.
Mar 1885-1958: PRO Chancery Lane, RG33/154 (index in RG43/7, 11- 12).
Mar 1895-1924 and 1950-68: PRO Kew, FO441/1-35, 37.
Mar 1909: Guildhall Library, in Ms 11827.

Dardanelles
Births 1900-14: PRO Kew, FO733/1.

Edirne: see *Adrianople*

Istanbul: see *Constantinople*

Izmir: see *Smyrna*

Konieh (Konya)
Births 1895-1909: PRO Kew, FO732/1.

For addresses of repositories see page 2

For other sources which may relate to places on this page see 'How to use this guide' (page 1)

Smyrna (Izmir)
Bap 1795-1832, mar 1785 and 1797-1832, bur 1801-32: Guildhall Library, Ms 10446G (index in Ms 15061/1-2).
Births and baps 1800-1959, bur 1801-1958: Guildhall Library, Ms 29745.
Bap 1959-date, mar 1837-89, 1928-date, bur 1959-date: Smyrna Anglican Chaplaincy, details available from Guildhall Library.
Bap, mar and bur 1800-32: Society of Genealogists.
Bap, mar and bur 1833-49: PRO Chancery Lane, in RG33/155 (index to bap in RG43/1, mar in RG43/7, bur in RG43/3).

Note. For other places in the former Turkish empire see **BULGARIA, IRAQ, LEBANON, PALESTINE, ROUMANIA** and **SYRIA.**

UGANDA

Births, mar and deaths 1905-18: PRO Chancery Lane, in RG36 (index in RG43/18).
Bap and mar 1921-63: Society of Genealogists.
Mar 1898 in 'International memoranda' at Guildhall Library: see page 6.

UKRAINE

Nicolayeo, Odessa, Sebastopol and *Theodosia (Feodosiya):* see **RUSSIA**

UNITED STATES OF AMERICA

General
All original church registers are held locally in the United States, either in the churches themselves or in local repositories.

Civil registration records begin in the 1840s in a few American states, but in most states they do not begin until the late 19th or early 20th century. Details of these records, and addresses of state registration authorities, are given in G. B. Everton, *The Handy Book for Genealogists* (Logan, Utah, 1981) (not available at Guildhall Library).

For records of emigration to America see page 12.

For further information about American sources see Gilbert Harry Doane, *Searching for your Ancestors* (Minneapolis, 1973) (this book includes some details of the availability of civil registration records but does not give the location of individual church registers).

For addresses of repositories see page 2

For other sources which may relate to places on this page see 'How to use this guide' (page 1)

The following are available in the United Kingdom. Registers forwarded from British Consulates are listed first in alphabetical order. Other registers are arranged in alphabetical order by place under the appropriate state.

Aberdeen, British Consulate
Births 1916, deaths 1914: PRO Kew, FO700/22-3.

Boston, British Consulate
Births 1871-1932, deaths 1902-30: PRO Kew, FO706/1-3.

Cincinati, British Consulate
Births 1929, 1943-58, deaths 1947-55: PRO Kew, FO700/31-5.

Cleveland, British Consulate
Births 1914-69: PRO Kew, FO700/36-7, 39, 41-3.

Dallas, British Consulate
Births 1951-4, deaths 1951: PRO Kew, FO700/24-5.

Detroit, British Consulate
Births 1910-69, mar 1936-7, deaths 1931-68: PRO Kew, FO700/44-53.

El Paso, British Consulate
Births 1916-30, deaths 1914-26: PRO Kew, FO700/26-7.

Galveston, British Consulate
Births 1838-1918, deaths 1850-1927: PRO Kew, FO701/23-4.

Kansas City, British Consulate
Births 1904-22, 1944-66, mar 1958-61, deaths 1920-65: PRO Kew, FO700/54-60.

New Orleans, British Consulate
Births 1950-1932, mar 1852-81, deaths 1850-1932: PRO Kew, FO581/15-19.

Omaha, British Consulate
Births 1906: PRO Kew, FO700/61.

Pensacola, British Consulate
Births 1880-1901, deaths 1879-1905: PRO Kew, FO885/1-2.

Pittsburgh, British Consulate
Births 1954-6: PRO Kew, FO700/62-3.

For addresses of repositories see page 2

For other sources which may relate to places on this page see 'How to use this guide' (page 1)

Portland (Oregan), British Consulate
Births 1880-1926, deaths 1929: PRO Kew, FO707/1-2

Providence, British Consulate
Births 1902-30, deaths 1930: PRO Kew, FO700/8-9.

St Louis, British Consulate
Births 1902-69, mar 1913-68, deaths 1913-66: PRO Kew, FO739/11-13, 15-17.

St Paul, British Consulate
Births 1943-66, deaths 1944: PRO Kew, FO700/71-4.

Tacoma, British Consulate
Births 1896-1921, deaths 1892-1907: PRO Kew, FO700/20-1.

Washington, British Legation
Mar 1828 in 'International memoranda' at Guildhall Library: see page 6.

Alabama, Lawrence County
Mar 1820-35: Society of Genealogists.

California, Anaheim
Bur 1880-1918: Society of Genealogists.

California, Butte County
Mar 1851-60: Society of Genealogists.

California, Capistrano
Bap 1780-1854, mar 1842-1924, bur 1831-1928: Society of Genealogists.

California, Colusa County
Mar 1853-60: Society of Genealogists.

California, El Dorado County
Mar 1844-60: Society of Genealogists.

California, Mendocino County
Mar 1859-60: Society of Genealogists.

California, Napa County
Mar 1850-77, deaths 1873-1905: Society of Genealogists.

For addresses of repositories see page 2

For other sources which may relate to places on this
page see 'How to use this guide' (page 1)

California, Nevada County
Mar 1854-61: Society of Genealogists.

California, Orange County
Births 1889-1912, mar 1890-8, deaths 1889-1906: Society of Genealogists.

California, Placer County
Mar 1851-60: Society of Genealogists.

California, Plumas County
Mar 1854-9: Society of Genealogists.

California, Sacramento County
Mar 1850-60: Society of Genealogists.

California, Santa Ana
Presbyterian bap 1881-1905: Society of Genealogists.

California, Santa Barbara County
Index to mar 1878-84: Society of Genealogists.
Mar 1885-1914: Society of Genealogists.

California, Shasta County
Mar 1852-60: Society of Genealogists.

California, Siskiyou County
Mar 1852-60: Society of Genealogists.

California, Solano County
Mar 1850-8: Society of Genealogists.

California, Sonoma County
Mar 1844-60: Society of Genealogists.

California, Sonora
Bur 1852-91: Society of Genealogists.

California, Sutter County
Mar 1850-60: Society of Genealogists.

For addresses of repositories see page 2

For other sources which may relate to places on this
page see 'How to use this guide' (page 1)

California, Tehama County
Mar 1854-60: Society of Genealogists.

California, Trinity County
Mar 1857-60: Society of Genealogists.

California, Tuolumne County
Births 1858-88, mar 1852-79, deaths 1894-1915: Society of Genealogists.

California, Yolo County
Mar 1850-60: Society of Genealogists.

California, Yuba County
Mar 1850-60: Society of Genealogists.

Colorado
Mar 1866-81: Society of Genealogists.

Colorado, Baca County
Mar 1889-99: Society of Genealogists.

Colorado, Boulder County
Mar 1863-84: Society of Genealogists.

Colorado, Conejus
Roman Catholic mar 1860-81: Society of Genealogists.

Colorado, Denver
Methodist bap 1861-1903, mar 1861-85: Society of Genealogists.
Bur extracts 1870-1908: Society of Genealogists.

Colorado, Douglas County
Mar 1909-17: Society of Genealogists.

Colorado, Jefferson County
Mar 1868-81: Society of Genealogists.

Colorado, Kit Carson County
Mar 1890-1929: Society of Genealogists.

Colorado, Littleton
Bur 1864-1907: Society of Genealogists.

For addresses of repositories see page 2

For other sources which may relate to places on this
page see 'How to use this guide' (page 1)

Colorado, Prowers County
Mar 1889-94: Society of Genealogists.

Colorado, Weld County
Mar 1881-2: Society of Genealogists.

Connecticut
Mar to 1699: Society of Genealogists.

Connecticut, Ashford
Mar 1750-1850, deaths to 1850 (extracts): Society of Genealogists.
Congregational bap, mar and deaths 1768-1937: Society of Genealogists.

Connecticut, Avon
Deaths to 1850: Society of Genealogists.
Congregational bap, mar and deaths 1798-1921: Society of Genealogists.

Connecticut, Barkhamstead
Deaths to 1850: Society of Genealogists.

Connecticut, Berlin
Deaths to 1850: Society of Genealogists.

Connecticut, Bethlehem
Deaths to 1850: Society of Genealogists.

Connecticut, Bolton
Deaths to 1850: Society of Genealogists.

Connecticut, Bozram
Deaths to 1850: Society of Genealogists.

Connecticut, Branford
Deaths to 1850: Society of Genealogists.

Connecticut, Bristol
Deaths to 1850: Society of Genealogists.

Connecticut, Brookfield
Deaths to 1850: Society of Genealogists.

For addresses of repositories see page 2

For other sources which may relate to places on this
page see 'How to use this guide' (page 1)

Connecticut, Brooklyn
Deaths to 1850: Society of Genealogists.

Connecticut, Clinton
Deaths to 1809-78: Society of Genealogists.

Connecticut, Farmington: see *Connecticut, Avon*

Connecticut, Groton
Index to mar 1749-85: Society of Genealogists.

Connecticut, Middletown
Births 1730-1850: Society of Genealogists.

Connecticut, New London
Mar extracts to 1850: Society of Genealogists.

Connecticut, North Haven
Congregational bap 1760-89: Society of Genealogists.

Connecticut, Pomfret
Bur extracts 1780-1839: Society of Genealogists.

Connecticut, Stonington
Births to 1730: Society of Genealogists.

Connecticut, Stratford
Births extracts to 1730: Society of Genealogists.

Connecticut, Westford: see *Connecticut, Ashford*

Connecticut, Wethersfield
Births to 1850: Society of Genealogists.

Delaware
Mar to 1699: Society of Genealogists.

Delaware, New Castle County
Births 1810-53: Society of Genealogists.

For addresses of repositories see page 2

For other sources which may relate to places on this
page see 'How to use this guide' (page 1)

District of Columbia, Washington
Episcopalian births and deaths 1791-1806: Society of Genealogists.
Jewish bur 1856-1919: Society of Genealogists.

Georgia, Milledgeville
Index to mar 1806-42: Society of Genealogists.

Indiana, Wayne County
Mar 1811-30: Society of Genealogists.

Kentucky, Campbell County
Mar 1808-10: Society of Genealogists.

Kentucky, Florence
Indexes to Lutheran bap 1811-42, mar 1835-42: Society of Genealogists.

Kentucky, Scott County
Index to mar 1793-1831: Society of Genealogists.

Kentucky, Shelby County
Mar 1792-1800: Society of Genealogists.

Louisiana, Arcadia
Mar extracts 1896-1912: Society of Genealogists.

Louisiana, Avoyelles: see *Louisiana, Hessmer*

Louisiana, Baton Rouge
Mar extracts 1841-79: Society of Genealogists.

Louisiana, Brusly: see *Louisiana, Baton Rouge*

Louisiana, Cornerview: see *Louisiana, New River*

Louisiana, Destrehan
Bap 1741-55, deaths 1739-55 (extracts): Society of Genealogists.

Louisiana, Hessmer
Bur 1922-48: Society of Genealogists.

Louisiana, Iberville
Mar 1788-1820: Society of Genealogists.

For addresses of repositories see page 2

For other sources which may relate to places on this
page see 'How to use this guide' (page 1)

Louisiana, Jackson
Mar extracts 1880-1910: Society of Genealogists.

Louisiana, Lakeland
Bap 1873-84, mar 1873-91, bur 1883-99: Society of Genealogists.

Louisiana, Morganza
Mar 1786-1842: Society of Genealogists.

Louisiana, New Orleans
Bap 1729-1845, mar 1731-1837, bur 1724-1848: Society of Genealogists.
Episcopalian bap, mar and deaths 1849-1900 (extracts): Society of Genealogists.
Bap, mar and bur 1841-3 (extracts): Society of Genealogists.
Indexes to some bap 1838-73, mar 1833-1907; Society of Genealogists.
Irish mar 1806-59: Society of Genealogists.

Louisiana, New River
Indexes to bap 1863-82, mar 1864-94, bur 1863-1908: Society of Genealogists.

Louisiana, Opelousas
Mar 1807-15: Society of Genealogists.

Louisiana, Paincourtville
Index to bap 1844-9, mar 1839-48: Society of Genealogists.

Louisiana, Plattenville
Index to mar 1817-80: Society of Genealogists.

Louisiana, St Charles
Mar 1883-9: Society of Genealogists.

Louisiana, St James
Bap 1757-87, mar 1770-81, bur 1773-83: Society of Genealogists.

Louisiana, St Martinville
Episcopalian bap 1870-1902: Society of Genealogists.

Louisiana, Tensas
Mar 1861-6: Society of Genealogists.

For addresses of repositories see page 2

For other sources which may relate to places on this page see 'How to use this guide' (page 1)

Louisiana, Trebonne
Index to mar extracts 1814-99: Society of Genealogists.

Louisiana, Vacherie
Index to bap 1856-63, mar 1856-85: Society of Genealogists.

Louisiana, Violet
Index to bap and mar extracts 1801-64: Society of Genealogists.
Bap 1873-6: Society of Genealogists.
Index to bur 1854-9: Society of Genealogists.

Maine
Mar to 1699: Society of Genealogists.

Maryland
Mar 1634-1777: printed in R. Barnes, *Maryland Marriages* (Baltimore, 1975).
Mar to 1777 (as above): Society of Genealogists.

Maryland, Baltimore County
Black mar 1778-1846: Society of Genealogists.

Maryland, Frederick County
Bap 1728-81, mar 1743-75: Society of Genealogists.

Maryland, Thurmont
Lutheran and Reformed bap 1773-1848: Society of Genealogists.

Massachusetts
Mar to 1699: Society of Genealogists.

Massachusetts, Barnstable
Births, mar and deaths 1642-1807: Leonard H. Smith, *Vital Records of Southeastern Massachusetts* vol 3 (Clearwater, Florida, 1982).

Massachusetts, Boston
Bap 1738-1830, mar 1737-1829, bur 1739-1829: Society of Genealogists.

Massachusetts, Bradford
Births, mar and deaths to 1849: Society of Genealogists.

Massachusetts, Cambridge
Bap 1658-1839, mar 1701-1831, deaths 1783-1830: Society of Genealogists.

For addresses of repositories see page 2

For other sources which may relate to places on this
page see 'How to use this guide' (page 1)

Massachusetts, Danvers
Births, mar and deaths to 1849: Society of Genealogists.

Massachusetts, Dedham
Bap 1635-1845, deaths 1637-1720: Society of Genealogists.

Massachusetts, Eastham and Orleans
Births, mar and deaths 1643-1842: Leonard H. Smith, *Vital Records of Southeastern Massachusetts* vol 1 (Clearwater, Florida, 1980).

Massachusetts, Fairhaven
Births, mar and deaths c.1733-c.1881: Leonard H. Smith, *Vital Records of Southeastern Massachusetts* vol 4 (Clearwater, Florida, 1986).

Massachusetts, Groton
Births, mar and deaths to 1849: Society of Genealogists.

Massachusetts, Ipswich
Births, mar and deaths to 1849: Society of Genealogists.

Massachusetts, Lancaster
Births, mar and deaths 1643-1850: Society of Genealogists.

Massachusetts, Marshfield
Births, mar and deaths to 1850: Society of Genealogists.

Massachusetts, Middleborough
Births, mar and deaths 1666-1807: Leonard H. Smith, *Vital Records of Southeastern Massachusetts* vol 2 (Clearwater, Florida, 1981).

Massachusetts, Orleans: see *Eastham and Orleans*

Massachusetts, Plymouth
Births, mar and deaths c.1663-c.1839: Leonard H. Smith, *Vital Records of Southeastern Massachusetts* vol 5 (Clearwater, Florida, 1989).
Bap 1724-87, deaths 1760-98: Society of Genealogists.
Mar to 1650: Society of Genealogists.

Massachusetts, Sandwich
Births, mar and deaths 1636-1775: Leonard H. Smith, *Vital Records of Southeastern Massachusetts* vol 3 (Clearwater, Florida, 1982).

For addresses of repositories see page 2

For other sources which may relate to places on this
page see 'How to use this guide' (page 1)

Massachusetts, Swansea
Births and mar 1663-1858, deaths 1663-1849, bur 1705-1805: Society of Genealogists.
Quaker mar 1733-1846: Society of Genealogists.

Massachusetts, Townsend
Births 1732-1851, mar 1734-1850, deaths 1732-1851: Society of Genealogists.

Massachusetts, Wareham
Births, bap, mar and deaths 1739-c.1891: Leonard H. Smith, *Records of the First Church of Wareham* . . . (Clearwater, Florida, 1974) and *Vital Records of Southeastern Massachusetts* vol 2 (Clearwater, Florida, 1981)

Michigan, Cass County
Mar 1850-73: Society of Genealogists.

Michigan, Detroit
German bap and mar 1835-47: Society of Genealogists.
Bur 1880-90: Society of Genealogists.

Michigan, Oakland County
Deaths 1867-75: Society of Genealogists.

Michigan, Pontiac
Bur 1869-1906: Society of Genealogists.

Michigan, Rose Township
Deaths and bur c.1837-1986: Society of Genealogists.

Michigan, Washtewaw County
Deaths extracts: 1867-74: Society of Genealogists.

Michigan, Wayne County
Deaths 1868-71: Society of Genealogists.

Michigan, West Bloomfield
Deaths 1897-1952, bur 1831-1988: Society of Genealogists.

Mississippi, Biloxi
Deaths, 1720-3: Society of Genealogists.

For addresses of repositories see page 2

For other sources which may relate to places on this page see 'How to use this guide' (page 1)

Mississippi, Natchez
Mar 1788-98: Society of Genealogists.

Missouri, Jackson County
Deaths 1883-4: Society of Genealogists.

Missouri, Kansas City
Deaths 1874-80: Society of Genealogists.

New Hampshire
Mar to 1699: Society of Genealogists.

New Hampshire, Hampton
Births and bap 1638-1900, mar and deaths 1654-1900: Society of Genealogists.

New Jersey
Mar to 1699: Society of Genealogists.

New Jersey, Basking Ridge
Bap 1795-1817: Society of Genealogists.

New Jersey, Belleville
Dutch Reformed bap 1727-94: Society of Genealogists.

New Jersey, Bergen
Dutch Reformed bap and mar 1789-1877, bur 1789-1810: Society of Genealogists.

New Jersey, Boundbrook
Presbyterian bap 1810-15: Society of Genealogists.

New Jersey, Burlington
Bap and mar 1703-1836, bur 1767-1836: Society of Genealogists.

New Jersey, Burlington County
Births 1753-73, mar 1782-94: Society of Genealogists.

New Jersey, Cape May
Baptist mar 1808-22: Society of Genealogists.

For addresses of repositories see page 2

For other sources which may relate to places on this page see 'How to use this guide' (page 1)

New Jersey, Cape May County
Mar 1807-17: Society of Genealogists.

New Jersey, Cheesequakes
Baptist mar 1798-1835: Society of Genealogists.

New Jersey, Cranbury
Presbyterian bap 1745-1833, mar 1790-1819: Society of Genealogists.

New Jersey, Daretown
Baptist mar 1772-93: Society of Genealogists.

New Jersey, Delaware
Episcopalian bap 1769-1823: Society of Genealogists.

New Jersey, Dumont
Dutch Reformed deaths 1783-1824: Society of Genealogists.

New Jersey, East Jersey
Mar 1666-88: Society of Genealogists.

New Jersey, Elizabeth
Episcopalian bap 1750-1826, mar 1751-87: Society of Genealogists.

New Jersey, Essex County
Mar 1795-1816: Society of Genealogists.

New Jersey, Fairfield
Dutch Reformed bap extracts 1741-8: Society of Genealogists.

New Jersey, Freehold and Middletown
Dutch Congregational bap 1709-1851, mar extracts 1736-1838: Society of
Genealogists.

New Jersey, Gloucester County
Mar to 1880: Society of Genealogists.

New Jersey, Greenwich
Lutheran bap 1770-1836: Society of Genealogists.

For addresses of repositories see page 2

For other sources which may relate to places on this
page see 'How to use this guide' (page 1)

New Jersey, Haddonfield
Quaker mar 1712-1808: Society of Genealogists.

New Jersey, Hamilton Square
Baptist mar 1837-54: Society of Genealogists.

New Jersey, Hunterdon County
Mar 1778-80: Society of Genealogists.
Baptist mar 1831-68: Society of Genealogists.

New Jersey, Kingston
Presbyterian bap 1792-1849, mar 1793-1850: Society of Genealogists.

New Jersey, Marlboro: see *New Jersey, Freehold and Middletown*

New Jersey, Mendham
Presbyterian bap 1805-32: Society of Genealogists.

New Jersey, Mercer County
Mar 1838-48: Society of Genealogists.

New Jersey, Metuchen
Presbyterian bap 1816-27, mar 1794-1822: Society of Genealogists.

New Jersey, Middletown
Baptist bap 1721-87, deaths 1786-1811: Society of Genealogists.
Mar 1684-99: Society of Genealogists.
See also: *New Jersey, Freehold and Middletown*

New Jersey, Monmouth County
Mar 1794-1849: Society of Genealogists.

New Jersey, Montgomery
Dutch Reformed bap 1727-1802, mar 1799-1802: Society of Genealogists.

New Jersey, Morris County
Mar 1795-1835: Society of Genealogists.

New Jersey, Morristown
Presbyterian bap 1746-1834, mar 1746-1844: Society of Genealogists.

For addresses of repositories see page 2

For other sources which may relate to places on this
page see 'How to use this guide' (page 1)

New Jersey, New Egypt
Methodist mar 1837-8: Society of Genealogists.

New Jersey, New Providence
Presbyterian bap 1764-97, mar 1763-96: Society of Genealogists.

New Jersey, Newark
Mar 1795-1807, bur 1795-1806: Society of Genealogists.

New Jersey, Newton
Mar 1684-1705: Society of Genealogists.

New Jersey, Oldwick
Lutheran mar 1770-1843: Society of Genealogists.

New Jersey, Piscataway
Births, mar and deaths 1668-1805, bur extracts 1789-1932: Society of Genealogists.

New Jersey, Plainfield: see *New Jersey, Rahway*

New Jersey, Pompton Plains
Dutch Reformed mar 1736-1809: Society of Genealogists.

New Jersey, Rahway and Plainfield
Quaker deaths 1705-1892: Society of Genealogists.

New Jersey, Salem County
Mar 1795-1809: Society of Genealogists.

New Jersey, Shrewsbury
Quaker births 1670-1883, mar 1674-1853, deaths and bur 1707-1896: Society of Genealogists.
Bap 1733-1824, mar 1691-1824, bur 1734-1824: Society of Genealogists.

New Jersey, Spotswood
Episcopalian bap 1788-1850, bur 1790-1850: Society of Genealogists.

New Jersey, Stillwater
Presbyterian bap 1806-50: Society of Genealogists.

For addresses of repositories see page 2

For other sources which may relate to places on this
page see 'How to use this guide' (page 1)

New Jersey, Sussex County
Mar 1777-1810: Society of Genealogists.

New Jersey, Washington
Presbyterian bap 1817-27, mar 1817-49: Society of Genealogists.

New Jersey, Walltown
Methodist bap 1812-15, mar 1807-27, bur 1806-27: Society of Genealogists.

New Jersey, West
Moravian bap 1742-62: Society of Genealogists.

New Jersey, Westfield
Presbyterian bap 1766-8, mar 1759-1803: Society of Genealogists.

New Jersey, Woodbridge
Births, mar and deaths 1668-1781: Society of Genealogists.

New York
Mar to 1699: Society of Genealogists.

New York, Amenia
Mar 1797-1803: Society of Genealogists.

New York, Athens: see *New York, Loonenburg*

New York, Ballston
Methodist bap 1877-1941, mar 1878-1941, bur 1880-1944: Society of Genealogists.

New York, Castleton
Slave births 1800-22: Society of Genealogists.

New York, Catskill
Dutch Reformed bap 1732-1800, mar 1732-1833: Society of Genealogists.

New York, Claverack
Bap 1727-1800, mar 1727-1929: Society of Genealogists.

New York, Courtlandtown
Dutch Reformed bap 1740-1830: Society of Genealogists.

For addresses of repositories see page 2

For other sources which may relate to places on this
page see 'How to use this guide' (page 1)

New York, Coxsackie
Dutch Reformed bap 1738-1800, mar 1797-1875: Society of Genealogists.

New York, Douglaston
Bap, mar and bur 1830-80: Society of Genealogists.

New York, Fishkill
Dutch Reformed mar 1731-1834: Society of Genealogists.

New York, Flushing
Episcopalian bap 1788-1853, mar 1782-1885, bur 1790-1896: Society of Genealogists.

New York, Goshen
Presbyterian bap 1773-1851, mar 1776-1885, deaths 1805-50: Society of Genealogists.

New York, Helderberg
Dutch Reformed mar 1794-1829: Society of Genealogists.

New York, Hopewell
Dutch Reformed mar 1766-1829: Society of Genealogists.

New York, Jamaica
Dutch Reformed bap 1702-1873, mar 1813-76, deaths 1835-98: Society of Genealogists.

New York, Jerusalem
Dutch Reformed mar 1794-1829: Society of Genealogists.

New York, Kakiat: see *New York, Tappan*

New York, Kings County
Slave births 1800-21: Society of Genealogists.

New York, Kingston
Dutch bap 1706-37, bur extracts 1739-95, bur 1805-16: Society of Genealogists.

For addresses of repositories see page 2

For other sources which may relate to places on this page see 'How to use this guide' (page 1)

New York, Loonenburg
Lutheran bap 1725-1800, mar 1705-83, deaths 1710-29: Society of Genealogists.

New York, Narragansett
French bap 1686-90, mar 1687-9, bur 1687-91: Society of Genealogists.

New York, New Salem
Dutch Reformed mar 1794-1829: Society of Genealogists.

New York, New Utrecht
Dutch Reformed bap 1718-99: Society of Genealogists.

New York, New York
Slave births 1799-1814: Society of Genealogists.
Dutch bap 1639-1800, mar 1639-1866, bur 1804-13: Society of Genealogists.
Lutheran bap 1725-83, mar 1752-91, bur 1704-85: Society of Genealogists.
Dutch Reformed bap 1739-1836, mar 1813-14, bur 1818-27: Society of Genealogists.
Bap 1784-1842, mar 1748-1861, deaths 1795-1842: Society of Genealogists.
Bap extracts 1787-1800: Society of Genealogists.
Presbyterian bap 1808-59, mar 1868-92: Society of Genealogists.
Episcopalian bap, mar and bur 1843-53: Society of Genealogists.
Baptist mar 1866-87: Society of Genealogists.

New York, Oyster Bay: see *New York, Wolver Hollow*

New York, Poughkeepsie
Dutch Reformed mar 1746-1835: Society of Genealogists.
See also: *New York, Rumbout and Poughkeepsie*

New York, Princetown
Dutch Reformed mar 1794-1850: Society of Genealogists.

New York, Redhook: see *New York, Rhinebeck Flats*

New York, Rhinebeck Flats
Dutch Reformed bap 1730-1800: Society of Genealogists.

New York, Rotterdam
Reformed bap 1800-38: Society of Genealogists.

For addresses of repositories see page 2

For other sources which may relate to places on this page see 'How to use this guide' (page 1)

New York, Rumbout and Poughkeepsie
Presbyterian mar 1825-46: Society of Genealogists.

New York, Saugerties
Dutch bap 1802-15, mar 1735-1872: Society of Genealogists.

New York, Schenectady
Dutch Reformed mar 1694-1768: Society of Genealogists.

New York, Shawangunk
Dutch Reformed mar 1789-1816: Society of Genealogists.

New York, Tappan
Dutch Reformed bap 1767-78, mar 1699-1831: Society of Genealogists.

New York, Western
Mar 1805-26: Society of Genealogists.

New York, Wolver Hollow
Dutch Reformed bap 1741-1834: Society of Genealogists.

New York, Yonkers
Episcopalian bap 1820-6, mar 1820-40, deaths 1820-6: Society of Genealogists.

North Carolina
Mar to 1699: Society of Genealogists.

North Carolina, Durham County
Mar 1881-1906: Society of Genealogists.

North Carolina, Flat Rock
Bap 1840-93, mar 1855-92, bur 1847-1923: Society of Genealogists.

Ohio, Cincinnati
Presbyterian bap 1811-40: Society of Genealogists.

Pennsylvania
Mar 1685-1810: printed in *Record of Pennsylvania Marriages prior to 1810* (anon.; Baltimore, 1968) (not available at Guildhall Library).

For addresses of repositories see page 2

For other sources which may relate to places on this
page see 'How to use this guide' (page 1)

Mar c.1742-90: printed in J. B. Linn and W. H. Egle, *Pennsylvania Marriages prior to 1790* (Baltimore, 1976) (not available at Guildhall Library).

Pennsylvania, Abington
Presbyterian mar 1716-1821: Society of Genealogists.

Pennsylvania, Albany
Lutheran and Reformed bap 1768-1863: Society of Genealogists.

Pennsylvania, Bensalem
Dutch Reformed bap 1710-38: Society of Genealogists.

Pennsylvania, Bethlehem
Moravian mar 1742-1800: Society of Genealogists.

Pennsylvania, Bern
Dutch Reformed Congregational bap 1738-1835: Society of Genealogists.

Pennsylvania, Buckingham
Quaker mar 1730-1810: Society of Genealogists.

Pennsylvania, Carlisle
Presbyterian mar 1785-1812: Society of Genealogists.

Pennsylvania, Chester
Episcopalian mar 1704-33: Society of Genealogists.

Pennsylvania, Churchville
Presbyterian mar 1738-1810: Society of Genealogists.

Pennsylvania, Derry: see *Pennsylvania, Paxtang and Derry.*

Pennsylvania, Emaus
Moravian mar 1758-1800: Society of Genealogists.

Pennsylvania, Flakner Swamp
Reformed mar 1748-1800: Society of Genealogists.

Pennsylvania, Falls
Quaker mar 1700-1800: Society of Genealogists.

For addresses of repositories see page 2

For other sources which may relate to places on this page see 'How to use this guide' (page 1)

Pennsylvania, Heidelberg
Reformed bap 1745-1805: Society of Genealogists.

Pennsylvania, Litiz
Moravian mar 1743-1800: Society of Genealogists.

Pennsylvania, Loretto
Roman Catholic bap and mar 1799-1840, deaths 1793-1899: Society of Genealogists.

Pennsylvania, Middletown
Quaker mar 1685-1810: Society of Genealogists.

Pennsylvania, Mifflin
Lutheran mar 1824-6: Society of Genealogists.

Pennsylvania, Nazareth
Moravian mar 1742-1800: Society of Genealogists.

Pennsylvania, Neshaminy
Presbyterian mar 1785-1804: Society of Genealogists.

Pennsylvania, New Hanover
Lutheran mar 1745-1809: Society of Genealogists.

Pennsylvania, Newtown
Mar 1798-1809: Society of Genealogists.

Pennsylvania, Paxtang and Derry
Mar 1741-1810: Society of Genealogists.

Pennsylvania, Perkiomen
Episcopalian mar 1788-1810: Society of Genealogists.

Pennsylvania, Philadelphia
Quaker mar 1682-1756: Society of Genealogists.
Presbyterian mar 1702-1812: Society of Genealogists.
Mar 1709-1806: Society of Genealogists.
Moravian mar 1743-1800: Society of Genealogists.
German Reformed mar 1748-1802: Society of Genealogists.
Swedish mar 1750-1810: Society of Genealogists.
Baptist mar 1761-1803: Society of Genealogists.

For addresses of repositories see page 2

For other sources which may relate to places on this page see 'How to use this guide' (page 1)

Pennsylvania, Quakertown
Quaker mar 1752-1810: Society of Genealogists.

Pennsylvania, Weisenburg
Mar 1790-1810, bur 1790-5: Society of Genealogists.

Rhode Island
Mar to 1699: Society of Genealogists.

South Carolina
Mar to 1699: Society of Genealogists.

South Carolina, Charleston
Bap 1754-1810, mar 1755-1802, bur 1753-1803: Society of Genealogists.

South Carolina, Georgetown
Methodist bap and mar 1811-37, deaths 1816-56: Society of Genealogists.

Tennessee, Rutherford County
Mar extracts 1824-71: Society of Genealogists.

Texas, Cherokee County
Index to births 1872-5: Society of Genealogists.

Texas, Clay County
Index to mar 1876-91: Society of Genealogists.

Texas, Fluvanna County
Mar 1781-1849: Society of Genealogists.

Texas, San Augustine
Mar 1837-46: Society of Genealogists.

Utah, Salt Lake City
Bur 1848-56: Society of Genealogists.

Vermont, Bennington
Mar extracts 1809-28: Society of Genealogists.

Virginia
Quaker birth extracts 1668-1717, mar 1682-1728, deaths and bur 1674-1723:

For addresses of repositories see page 2

For other sources which may relate to places on this
page see 'How to use this guide' (page 1)

Society of Genealogists.
Mar to 1699: Society of Genealogists.

Virginia, Alexandria
Episcopalian bap, mar and bur 1809-61 (extracts): Society of Genealogists.

Virginia, Bristol
Births 1720-92: Society of Genealogists.

Virginia, Campbell County
Mar 1800-10: Society of Genealogists.

Virginia, Farnham
Bap extracts 1672-1781: Society of Genealogists.

Virginia, Fredericksburg
Mar extracts 1782-1860: Society of Genealogists.

Virginia, Gretna
Births, mar and deaths 1730-1844: Society of Genealogists.

Virginia, Loudon County
Mar 1757-1853: Society of Genealogists.

Virginia, Madison
Lutheran births 1750-1825: Society of Genealogists.

Virginia, Middlesex County
Bap 1653-1812, mar and bur 1660-1812: printed in *The Parish Register of Christchurch, Middlesex County, Virginia* (anon., Richmond, Virginia, 1897) (not available at Guildhall Library).

Virginia, Monongalia County
Mar 1795-1812: Society of Genealogists.

Virginia, Orange County
Mar 1772-1810: Society of Genealogists.

Virginia, Rockingham
Bap 1791-1832: Society of Genealogists.

For addresses of repositories see page 2

For other sources which may relate to places on this
page see 'How to use this guide' (page 1)

Virginia, St Paul's
Bap 1725-73, mar 1716-93 (extracts): Society of Genealogists.

Virginia, Surry County
Mar extracts 1679-1791: Society of Genealogists.

Virginia, York County
Bap 1648-1789, bur 1665-1787: printed in L. C. Bell, *Charles Parish, York County, Virginia: History and Registers* (Richmond, Virginia, 1932) (not available at Guildhall Library).

West Virginia, Aurora
Lutheran bap 1792-1812: Society of Genealogists.

Wisconsin, St Croix County
Mar 1852-67: Society of Genealogists.

Note. Assistance in tracing other registers may be obtainable from local genealogical societies in the United States, whose addresses can be found in Mary Keysor (ed.), *Meyer's Directory of Genealogical Societies in the U.S.A. and Canada* (Mount Airy, Maryland, 1990). Microfilm copies of many genealogical records are held by the Genealogical Society of the Church of Latter-Day Saints, Family History Centre, 35 North West Temple Street, Salt Lake City, Utah 84150.

URUGUAY

Fray Bentos
Mar 1871-92: Guildhall Library, Ms 11223.

Montevideo
Bap 1843, mar 1881-90 in 'International memoranda' at Guildhall Library: see page 6.

VENEZUELA

Bap 1843-7, births 1850, deaths 1817, bur 1843 in 'International memoranda' at Guildhall Library: see page 6.
Mar 1836-8: PRO Chancery Lane, in RG33/155 (index in RG43/7).

VIRGIN ISLANDS: see WEST INDIES

For addresses of repositories see page 2

For other sources which may relate to places on this page see 'How to use this guide' (page 1)

WEST INDIES

General
Some register transcripts of former British colonies in the West Indian islands are available in the United Kingdom (see below), but all original church registers are held locally in the West Indies.

The Society of Genealogists holds a number of sources relating to the West Indies. They are described in detail in Anthony J. Camp, *Sources for Anglo-West Indian Genealogy in the Library of the Society of Genealogists* (to be published).

For records of emigration to the West Indies see page 12.

Anguilla
For registers (from 1826) held locally see E. C. Baker, *A Guide to Records in the Leeward Islands* (Oxford, 1965).

Antigua
Bap 1689-1860, mar 1690-1850, bur 1689-1837: Society of Genealogists.
Bap 1725-1864, mar 1686-1885, bur 1686-1860 (extracts): Society of Genealogists.
Bap 1733-4 and 1738-45, mar 1745, bur 1733-4 and 1738-45: PRO Kew, in CO152/21,25; printed in *Caribbeana* vol 1 (1910).
Bap 1770-1830, mar 1710-1841, bur 1691-1839: extracts printed in *Miscellanea Genealogica et Heraldica* 2nd series vol 4 (1892).
For registers (from 1689) held locally see E. C. Baker, *A Guide to Records in the Leeward Islands* (Oxford, 1965).

Bahamas
Bap 1721-8, mar and bur 1723-8: Lambeth Palace Library, in Fulham Papers vol 15. Microfilm copy available at Guildhall Library, Microfilm 372.
Bap 1813-16, mar 1811 in 'International memoranda' at Guildhall Library: see page 6.
For registers (from 1744) held locally see D. Gail Saunders and E. A. Carson, *Guide to the Records of the Bahamas* (Nassau, Bahamas, 1973).

Barbados
Bap 1637-1800: printed in Joanne McRee Sanders, *Barbados Records* (Baltimore, 1984)
Bap 1637-1800 (as above): Society of Genealogists.
Mar 1643-1800: printed in Joanne McRee Sanders, *Barbados Records* (Houston, Texas, 1982).

For addresses of repositories see page 2

For other sources which may relate to places on this page see 'How to use this guide' (page 1)

Mar 1643-1800 (as above): Society of Genealogists.
Mar 1643-1700: British Library, Add Ms 38825.
Mar 1648-52: printed in *Caribbeana* vol 1 (1910).
Bap and bur 1678-9: PRO Kew, in CO1/44; printed in J. C. Hotten, *The Original Lists of Persons . . . who went from Great Britain to the American Plantations* (New York, 1931). Another copy: Guildhall Library, Ms 2202/1.
Mar and deaths 1783-9: printed in *Caribbeana* vol 3 (1914).
Births, mar and deaths 1805-18: printed in *Caribbeana* Vol 1-2 (1910-12).
Methodist mar 1830-4 and 1857-86: Methodist Missionary Society.
For registers (from 1637) held locally enquiries should be addressed to the Department of Archives, Black Rock, St Michael, Barbados, West Indies. See C. J. Stanford, 'Genealogical Sources in Barbados', in *Genealogists' Magazine* vol 17 no 9 (1974).

Cuba
Mar 1842-9: PRO Chancery Lane, in RG33/155 (index in RG43/7).

Dominica
For registers (from 1730) held locally see E. C. Baker, *A Guide to Records in the Windward Islands* (Oxford, 1968).

Dominican Republic, Cuidad Trujillo (Santo Domingo)
Births 1868-1932, mar 1921-8, bur 1849-1910, deaths 1874-89: PRO Kew, FO683/3-4, 6.
Mar 1849, 1868: PRO Kew, FO140/8.

Grenada
For registers (from 1784) held locally see E. C. Baker, *A Guide to Records in the Windward Islands* (Oxford, 1968).

Guadeloupe
Military bap 1813-14, mar 1813-15, bur 1813-14: extracts printed in *The Genealogist* vol 1 (1877), and re-printed in *Caribbeana* vol 1 (1910). The original vol from which these extracts were taken is now part of the Registrar General's military records held by the Office of Population Censuses and Surveys (see page 9).
Bap, mar, bur 1813-16 (as above): Society of Genealogists.

Haiti
Births 1833-50, mar 1833-93, deaths 1833-50: PRO Kew, FO866/14, 21-2.

For addresses of repositories see page 2

For other sources which may relate to places on this page see 'How to use this guide' (page 1)

Haiti, Aux Cayes
Births 1870-1905, deaths 1871-1907: PRO Kew, FO376/1-2.

Jamaica
Births 1814-48, mar and deaths 1779-1848: Guildhall Library Printed Books Section, typescript entitled 'A collection of extracts from Jamaican and other newspapers relating to Jamaican families' (c.1930).
Mar 1666-79: British Library, Add Ms 21931; printed in *Caribbeana* vol 1 (1910).
Mar and deaths 1796-1800: printed in *Caribbeana* vol 4 (1916).
For registers (from 1664) held locally enquiries should be addressed to the Registrar General, General Register Office, Spanish Town PO, St Catherine, Jamaica, West Indies..

Montserrat
Bap 1721-9 and 1739-45, mar 1721-9, bur 1721-9 and 1739-45: PRO Kew, in CO152/18,25; printed in *Caribbeana* vol 1 (1910).
Bap and mar 1721-9, mar 1721-8; Society of Genealogists.
For registers (from 1771) held locally see E. C. Baker, *A Guide to Records in the Leeward Islands* (Oxford, 1965).

Nevis
Bap, mar and bur 1716-24: Lambeth Palace Library, in Fulham Papers vol 19. Microfilm copy available at Guildhall Library, Microfilm 374. Printed in Arthur Foley Winnington–Ingram and Sadler Phillips, *The Early English Colonies* (London, 1908); also (with omissions) in *Caribbeana* vol 2 (1912).
Bap and bur 1726-7, 1733-4 and 1740-5: PRO Kew, in CO152/16,21,25; printed in *Caribbeana* vol 1 (1910) and vol 4 (1916).
Bap 1729-33 and 1742-1800, mar 1729-37 and 1742-99, bur 1729-40 and 1742-99: printed in *Caribbeana* vol 1-3 (1910-1914).
For registers (from 1728) held locally see E. C. Baker, *A Guide to Records in the Leeward Islands* (Oxford, 1965).

St Christopher (St Kitts)
Bap 1719-1823, mar 1724-1821, bur 1719-1821: British Library, Add Mss 34181, 41178, 41295, 43743 and 43866.
Bap 1721-30, 1733-4 and 1738-45, mar 1733-4 and 1738-45, bur 1721-30, 1733-4 and 1738-45: PRO Kew, in CO152/18,21,25; printed in *Caribbeana* vol 1 (1910).
Bap 1729-1814, mar 1729-1832, bur 1729-1802: printed in Vere Langford Oliver, *Registers of St Thomas, Middle Island, St Kitts* (supplement to *Caribbeana* vol 4; London, 1915).

For addresses of repositories see page 2

For other sources which may relate to places on this page see 'How to use this guide' (page 1)

Bap 1732-1831, mar 1732-1828, bur 1733-1829: printed in *Caribbeana* vol 6 (1919).
Mar and deaths c.1755-1819: printed in *Caribbeana* vol 3 (1914).
Births, mar and deaths 1839-40: printed in *Caribbeana* vol 2 (1912).
For registers (from 1730) held locally see E. C. Baker, *A Guide to Records in the Leeward Islands* (Oxford, 1965).

St Kitts: see *St Christopher*

St Lucia
For registers (from 1770) held locally see E. C. Baker, *A Guide to Records in the Windward Islands* (Oxford, 1968).

St Vincent
For registers (from 1802) held locally see E. C. Baker, *A Guide to Records in the Windward Islands* (Oxford, 1968).

Tobago
Bap, mar and bur 1781-1817: printed in *Register of Baptisms, Marriages and Burials in the English Protestant Church, Tobago* (anon.; Port of Spain, Trinidad, 1936) (not available at Guildhall Library).
Bap, mar and bur 1781-1817 (as above): Society of Genealogists.

Trinidad
Births and bap 1851-2, mar 1850 in 'International memoranda' at Guildhall Library: see page 6.

Virgin Islands
For registers (from 1810) held locally in the British Virgin Islands see E. C. Baker, *A Guide to Records in the Leeward Islands* (Oxford, 1965).
Many entries for the Danish (later U.S.) Virgin Islands among registrations for Denmark and its colonies in 'Miscellaneous' series 1826-1951 at PRO Chancery Lane (see page 9).

YUGOSLAVIA
Some bap post 1920 in the Bishop of Gibraltar's memorandum book at Guildhall Library: see page 6.

For addresses of repositories see page 2

For other sources which may relate to places on this page see 'How to use this guide' (page 1)
